RAKING THE HISTORIC COALS

WINSOR

DEWEY

POOLE

SMITH

THE COMMITTEE OF ARRANGEMENTS

EDWARD G. HOLLEY

RAKING THE HISTORIC COALS

THE A.L.A. SCRAPBOOK OF 1876

BETA PHI MU 1967

B Φ M Chapbook Number Eight

Copyright© B Φ M 1967

Library of Congress card number 67–28354

This is the eighth in a series of chapbooks published by Beta Phi Mu, national library science honorary fraternity, as a contribution to the art of book design and the literature of books and libraries.

Of the seven previous authors in the series, two have been librarians, and the fraternity is again privileged to present the work of one of its members, Edward G. Holley, director of libraries at the University of Houston. Dr. Holley has won several accolades, including the Scarecrow Press Award for Library Literature for his *Charles Evans, American Bibliographer*, published in 1963. He is also a regular contributor to professional journals on subjects ranging from university libraries to the problems of a biographer.

Designer for this chapbook is A. Doyle Moore, with an assist from Kim Merker. A. Doyle Moore is a professor of art at the University of Illinois with a special interest in paper making, book design, type faces, bookbinding, decorative end papers, antique printing presses, medieval drama, Plains Indians, concrete poetry and folk music. Kim Merker is the operator and sole proprietor of the celebrated Stone Wall Press of Iowa City, a member of the faculty of the University of Iowa, and the recipient of many honors for his contributions to the graphic arts.

For some, a profession's interest in the documents of its history is an indication of maturity. Others see such interest as a harmless, but quite unproductive, bit of antiquarianism. Something can be said for both points of view, but however one regards such documents, if he is a true professional, he cannot ignore them. They are the very essence of history and should be treated with respect.

In librarianship we pay considerable lip-service to "1876 and all that," as one of my colleagues has remarked, but few present day librarians know very much about what happened that year. They do know that the profession's accomplishments in 1876 were formidable and that they remain as a source of professional pride. After all, periodically the American Library Association has a celebration and announces that it is fifty, seventy-five, or ninety years old. Anyone who can subtract will come up with the correct date of organization. Too, those who love title pages and tables of contents can look at any issue of the *Library Journal*, most widely read of our professional magazines, and see that it was "Founded in 1876 by Melvil Dewey, R. R. Bowker, and Frederick Leypoldt."

Yet this is at best superficial knowledge. We know little about these men, their personalities, and the circumstances which brought the Association into existence. Some of us believe that a rekindling of the historic coals is long overdue. This book is an attempt to do precisely that by printing some of the basic documents relating to the founding of the American Library Association. Simply stated it is the story of the preparations for the 1876 meeting at which the American Library Association was born.

The idea for this volume came from a pleasant coffee break with Helen Welch at the University of Illinois in the spring of 1961. At that time I was working on my biography of Charles Evans, and, as usual, was bending the ear of anyone who would listen to my tale of progress (or the lack of it). That particular morning I described to Miss Welch some of the neglected items in library history which I had discovered. Among the items which attracted her always attentive ear was a scrapbook of letters, postcards, and printed documents called "Librarians' Conference, October, 1876," which I had seen at the A.L.A. Headquarters Library. Miss Welch immediately saw possibilities for publishing an edition of this scrapbook in the Beta Phi Mu chapbook series.

As the chief manuscript record of our professional history, the scrapbook obviously had more than sentimental value. Various discussions with Harold Lancour and D. A. Brown followed, and, eventually, I was asked to undertake the task of editing this scrapbook for publication. Mr. David Clift, Executive Director of the American Library Association, was somewhat skeptical, but gave his blessing to the project.

In the summer of 1963 I began serious work on the project and was permitted to take the original home to Texas where I could study it at my "leisure." For administrators, leisure is one of the commodities in shortest supply and the months have passed all too rapidly. The need for studying the background materials, the long and sometimes fruitless search for manuscripts of some of the major participants, and even the dating of an individual's period of librarianship at a given institution have conspired to slow the rate of progress. At last there was only one thing to do: in the words of the late Walter Prescott Webb: "Write the damn thing now."

What is the 1876 scrapbook, the substance of which we offer between these boards? The scrapbook itself consists of 216 items, mostly autograph letters, beginning with Justin Winsor's response of May 18, 1876, to a Dewey-Leypoldt letter about supporting a conference and concluding with the advance proofs from the first issue of the *American Library Journal* which described the Conference program for the meeting in Philadelphia, October 4-6, 1876. These letters reflect the library questions being discussed at the time, certain conflicts among the leading personalities, and the broad base of interest in organization of the profession. Some of the letters and postcards are routine: "Yes, I'll attend the conference; send me a program," but others have considerably more substance.

How did it come about that these letters were preserved? Melvil Dewey, the Conference Secretary, and Justin Winsor, the Chairman, apparently kept many of the letters they received. Someone at the Boston Public Library later pasted these into a scrapbook and bound them into a volume in 1877, with a pencilled title page, "Librarians Conference Oct. 1876 Letters, etc." In blue pencil, on the first page is the accession number, 232962, and a date, July 28, 1877-. The volume has been rebound, with the additional word on the spine, "American Library Association 1926." On the last page has been pasted an attested true copy of a resolution of the Board of Trustees, dated July 16, 1926, "VOTED: that the Director be authorized to transfer to the custody of the American Library Association, a collection of letters and other documents now in the Library files, relating to the first meeting of the Association held at Philadelphia in 1876." This copy is signed by Charles Belden, then Director of the Boston Public Library and also President of the American Library Association.

This, then, is the history of the American Library Association's historical scrapbook. Melvil Dewey and Justin Winsor collected and preserved certain letters. In 1877 they were placed in a scrapbook where they slumbered for the next fifty years. To enhance the nostalgia of the fiftieth anniversary conference, Mr. Belden persuaded the trustees to have the scrapbook rebound, and turned over to the American Library Association for the headquarter's archives. Another twenty-five years passed until William L. Williamson, then working on his biography of William F. Poole, made a careful examination, and became interested in its contents. When I first met Mr. Williamson in 1959, he suggested that I have a look at the scrapbook to check the Evans' letters. His description of its location was vivid: access to the room where it was kept was through the men's room in the old Cyrus McCormick mansion, then the A.L.A. headquarters. I quickly followed Mr. Williamson's advice, and my first impression was, and still remains, "How persistent are the issues which trouble librarianship!" Let me add that when I picked up the scrapbook at the close of the 1963 conference in Chicago it was reposing in an exhibit case containing some of the primary documents relating to the Association's history. From washroom to "watch-room," you might say.

The limits of this book are the limits of the scrapbook itself: May to October, 1876. It is a book about the *preparations* for the conference itself. Out of 216 items in the scrapbook, 74, or about one-third, are included here. Many of the letters simply endorsed the idea or asked for an invitation or program. Only representative samples of such letters are included. On the other hand, most letters containing concrete suggestions for conference discussion, or relating to the major conference figures, have been reproduced. To supplement the scrapbook itself I have sought additional documents from other sources. Some 26 such items appear and their location is identified in the notes. Thus we present here a total of 100 documents. Where no location is given, the item is from the scrapbook itself.

The letters and other documents have been arranged in chronological order to tell the story by themselves, with enough in the way of explanatory notes to identify persons and places if known. The sense of continuity has perhaps been improved by the articles and notes of the articulate Charles Ammi Cutter from *The Nation*. The items reproduced are exact transcriptions, with a few commas added occasionally to help the reader. Citations are given in full the first time they appear and in abbreviated form thereafter. It is with regret that I have excluded some conference items, especially John William Wallace's opening address. My regret has been tempered by the G. K. Hall Company's publication of the latter as it's Christmas booklet for 1965. One must draw a line, however, and the conference itself will have to await another historian and another book.

The English librarian Stanley Jast is reported to have said that librarians as a class are much too bashful. "He observed that most of the town librarians who had crossed the library stage since public libraries began were quiet lads who had done their duty, taken their cash, and let the credit go. Only now and again had one stood out to catch the limelight of the stage, and quickly it would darken again."[1] Certainly anyone who has tried his hand at serious research into library history must agree with Mr. Jast. Nineteenth century librarians were, as Mr. Williamson says of Poole, men who were anxious to get on with the job. They were not concerned with future bright young men working on their dissertations or professional successors who wanted to re-create history "as it actually was." Yet both Poole and Justin Winsor held the presidency of the American Historical Association and wrote on historical subjects. Lloyd P. Smith, called the "hereditary librarian" of the Library Company of Philadelphia and a gentleman who believed in a solid classical background for librarianship, was scarcely unaware of the importance of historical documents. Still, our professional ancestors, deeply concerned about preserving the words and works of others, were strangely indifferent to the preservation of their own. We catch only glimpses of these men now and then through a letter, a speech, a report. Those glimpses are intriguing, revealing strong personalities, keen minds, and vigorous proponents of the value of books and libraries.

While this is scarcely the place to discuss library historiography, I cannot refrain from commenting upon the tragic loss of many of the

[1] *R. D. Macleod, "Who Was James Yates?"* Library Review, *no. 132* (*Winter, 1959*), *250*.

personal papers of men like Poole, Winsor, Cutter, Smith, and Spofford for the period covered. In seeking their letters from many repositories, only occasionally have I met with success. True, there are fewer letters of Winsor, Dewey, and Cutter because they were in Boston and could consult personally, but what about Winsor's letters to Poole and Spofford? As late as 1883 Poole still had most of his letters relating to the conference, but they have long since disappeared. There are all too many missing letters which would have added much to our picture of the conference preparations. Those of us who follow in the footsteps of these men are the poorer for their modesty.

In the often frustrating and maddening search for important letters I owe a debt to many people, but I must certainly mention the unfailing helpfulness of Mrs. Elizabeth L. Wright of the Boston Public Library, Mr. Robert W. Hill of the New York Public Library, and Mr. Kenneth A. Lohf of the Columbia University Libraries. Special thanks are due Dr. Godfrey Dewey, surviving son of Melvil Dewey, who came to my aid time and again in transcribing the cribbed shorthand (takigraphy) notes of his father which are written on some of the letters in the scrapbook.

Edward G. Holley
University of Houston

ACKNOWLEDGMENTS

Illustrations

Frontispiece:

Justin Winsor	Courtesy of the Trustees of the Boston Public Library
Melvil Dewey	Courtesy of the Columbia University Libraries
William F. Poole	Courtesy of William L. Williamson
Lloyd P. Smith	Courtesy of F. W. Faxon Company

Facsimiles of items 6, 18, 39, 71 all from the American Library Association's 1876 Scrapbook

Text

All items are from the American Library Association's 1876 Scrapbook except for the periodical articles as indicated and the following:

Items 2, 3, 10, 12, 13, 17, 27	Melvil Dewey Papers, Columbia University Libraries
Items 4, 5, 9, 11, 16, 22, 89	Superintendent's File, Boston Public Library
Items 62, 73	American Antiquarian Society
Items 72, 92	Charles Evans Papers, University of Illinois Library

Transcriptions of Melvil Dewey's shorthand notes by Dr. Godfrey Dewey

Abbreviations

AAS	American Antiquarian Society	Lbk	Letterbook
AL	Autograph letter	LJ	*Library Journal*
ALA	American Library Association	LS	Letter signed
ALJ	*American Library Journal*	NYPL	New York Public Library
ALS	Autograph letter signed		
BPL	Boston Public Library	PW	*Publishers' Weekly*
CUL	Columbia University Libraries	TD	Typed document
IUL	University of Illinois Library		

RAKING THE HISTORIC COALS

RAKING THE HISTORIC COALS

In his book, *The Emerging of Modern America*, Allan Nevins names 1876 as one of "two memorable years" in post-Civil War America. The nation had gone through a civil war, experienced a mire of scandals and political corruption perhaps not equaled in its history, and survived a debilitating financial panic. Moreover, the Hayes-Tilden election with its cliff-hanging results late in the year sorely tested the political faith of the country. Yet from all these stresses the nation had emerged with moderation and restraint, a remarkable testimonial, Nevins thinks, to the "steadfastness and orderliness of the American people."[1]

That same year, so significant as a time of testing for the United States, also saw the nation celebrate its centennial in a huge exhibition in Philadelphia. The emphasis was upon American achievement, and there was a new spirit in the air, an optimistic and courageous outlook for the future. Above all, educational activity at all levels beyond the elementary school was then receiving renewed attention. It was a time ripe for new ventures to match an expanding country.

From the viewpoint of the librarian, the year 1876 has further importance: it marked a turning point for American librarianship and the birth of the modern library profession. Despite the fact that public libraries had already expanded rapidly in the previous quarter of a century, librarians as yet had no professional organization through which they could communicate with each other. In October, 1876, the practitioners of the craft met in Philadelphia for "mutual consultation and practical co-operation," to promote "efficiency and economy in library work," and to present "plans for a permanent organization."[2] In looking back upon the year's work, an older librarian, with a hint of prophecy, remarked to Melvil Dewey, "Through all coming time 1876 will be looked upon as the most eventful year in the history of libraries—the year in which the librarian fairly claimed and received at the hands of the public his place among the recognized professions."[3]

Others echoed a similar sentiment, from the *Publishers' Weekly*, tireless advocate of library causes, to the journals of more general interest such as *Harper's* and *The Nation*. From across the Atlantic, Henry R. Tedder, Librarian of the Athenæum Club (London), speaking at the first International Conference of Librarians (1877), said that the year 1876 almost marked a "new period in the history of bibliothecal science"; and at the same conference, John Winter Jones of the British Museum acknowledged American librarianship's major contribution: "The idea of holding a Conference of Librarians originated in America—in that country of energy and activity which has set the world so many good examples, and of which a conference of Librarians is not the least valuable.... "[4]

In the perspective of history, 1876 was indeed a landmark year for the American librarian. Not only was his professional association organized, but the U. S. Bureau of Education published its massive survey, *Public Libraries in the United States of America*[5] (including the first edition of Cutter's *Rules for a Printed Dictionary Catalogue* as a separate part); and the *American Library Journal* began publication as the first professional library magazine. As if this were not enough, the year also saw the appearance of the first edition of Melvil Dewey's decimal classification and subject index, which was to sweep the field of classification and within the next two decades supersede most of the classification schemes then in existence. Never before or since have American librarians been able to claim as much fruition within a single twelve-month period.

In retrospect, it is a bit startling to realize that the name which was to become synonymous with librarianship, that of the energetic Melvil Dewey, held no magic power in 1876. One of the youngest men in the profession, Dewey had graduated only the year before from Amherst College and was virtually unknown among the practitioners of the period. The acknowledged Nestor of the profession, William Frederick Poole (then 55), is said to have been indignant at the presumption of this young man.[6] In later years Dewey liked to recall that he had started the American Library Association despite the opposition of one of the chief librarians of the period. He should not have limited himself to Poole. Another prominent librarian, Ainsworth Rand Spofford, Librarian of Congress, declined to lend his name to the project, "because I have always entertained insuperable objections to figuring in conventions (usually mere wordy outlets for impracticables and pretenders)."[7] He added that he looked "with distrust upon mixing the methods of the bibliographer, which are those of patient and accurate research, with the methods of the stump, which are conspicuously the reverse."[8] Dewey himself admitted, in a communication closer to the conference date, that "most of the leading librarians were doubtful of the possibil-

4

ity of accomplishing much," and that only Charles Ammi Cutter, of the Boston Athenæum, was pre-eminent among the hopeful.[9] All the same he had to add that the doubtful had become enthusiastic and worked side by side with the more confident. The singling out of Poole for special criticism came later.

This, however, is to jump ahead of the story. The point to be made here is that Melvil Dewey, despite his indisputable contributions later, was not a well-known figure at the beginning of the conference in 1876. This fact, initially, caused serious difficulties in securing the necessary backing of some leading librarians.

The 1876 library conference was not the first to be held in America. That distinction belongs to the conference of 1853, a gathering whose organization bears strong similarities to its successor twenty-three years later. Charles B. Norton, publisher of *Norton's Literary Gazette*, in the spring of 1853 began urging a library conference which his two editors, Seth Hastings Grant and Daniel Coit Gilman, had first publicized the year before.[10] Grant was then serving as Librarian of the New York Mercantile Library; and Gilman, later to make his mark as President of Johns Hopkins, had just graduated from Yale. Just which of the three —Norton, Grant or Gilman—actually wrote the editorial is unknown. At any rate, Norton's various editorials stimulated considerable interest; and an official call, signed by twenty-six librarians and bibliographers, was mailed in May.[11]

Eighty-two persons attended the conference in September, 1853, in New York City. The proceedings were dominated by Charles Coffin Jewett, then Assistant Secretary and Librarian of the Smithsonian Institution. At the time, Jewett was waging a losing battle with Dr. Joseph Henry, Secretary of the Smithsonian, over the proper way to disburse the institution's funds. He was a leading figure in the library world, and later served as Superintendent of the Boston Public Library from 1858 to 1868. Poole, who was a member of both conferences, said that "the Convention of 1853 made a lasting impression on the minds of all the librarians who were present and that it must be regarded as an era in American bibliography."[12]

From other accounts, too, the 1853 conference appears to have been highly successful. On the second day, Reuben A. Guild, Librarian of Brown University and another member of both conferences, introduced a resolution urging a permanent library organization with annual meetings.[13] The resolution was unanimously adopted, and many of the delegates confidently assumed, as they left for home, that a conference would be held the following year. Yet almost a quarter of a century intervened before another library conference was held. The reasons are probably varied, including the outbreak of the Civil War; but certainly among the chief reasons was the fact that Jewett was forced out of his position at the Smithsonian the following year. Too, Norton, the chief backer, met with financial reverses, and there was no one else to take the helm.

At this point it is pertinent to look at the development of other professions and their organizations during the nineteenth century. Perhaps the librarians had been premature in 1853. While it is true that the teachers had organized the National Education Association in 1851 and the American Association for the Advancement of Science had preceded the N.E.A. by three years, most professional associations came into existence after the Civil War. Furthermore, one might note that both the N.E.A. and the A.A.A.S. were broad discipline groups, with a rather inclusive patronage. More specialized groups such as the American Chemical Society (1876), the Modern Language Association (1883), the American Historical Association (1884), the American Economic Association (1885), and the Geological Society of America (1888) all date from the last quarter of the nineteenth century. In fact, a veritable flood of professional and scholarly associations came into being in the twenty-year period between 1876 and 1895. Both Arthur M. Schlesinger and Arthur E. Bestor, Jr., have discussed the formation of these associations in terms of the transformation of American scholarship and the expansion of learning in the post-Civil War period.[14] The impact of these currents on libraries was profound; and, given the rise of public libraries with the need for increased staffing and services, it would have been unusual for librarians not to have organized professionally during this period.

The idea of forming a library association, or at least the calling of a conference of librarians, did not spring full-blown from the head of Melvil Dewey in the spring of 1876 as has sometimes been asserted. Dewey's own hindsight in making such a claim is confusing. In response to an article on the origin of the Association which Bowker had published in January, 1896, Dewey stated that he had been at work on the idea of library development, including a plan for a national association, a library journal, and a library bureau, at least four years before he began his relationship with Bowker and Leypoldt at the *Publishers' Weekly* office in May, 1876. Even further down the road, in 1917, Dewey stated that the evolution of his plan occurred in 1875. Whatever the truth of the matter, Bowker's response to Dewey's claims in 1896 was that "on some of these points my remembrance is confirmatory of Mr. Dewey's and on others he speaks for himself,"[15] but he added that he did not want in any sense to deny Dewey due credit for the largest share in general library development.

As early as August, 1875, Thomas Hale Williams, Librarian of the Minneapolis Athenæum, had written to John Eaton, U.S. Commissioner of Education, suggesting the importance of a library convention and proposing a list of topics to be discussed. While the exact date of the Williams letter is uncertain, John Eaton did not reply until the following February.[16] He expressed regret at not having responded sooner and sent along letters from several chief librarians who had commented upon Williams' proposal. Unfortunately these letters have been lost. Why Williams, who was a member of the 1853 Conference, did not participate in the 1876 Conference is unknown, but he was having difficulties at home defending his policies at the Athenæum at about that time.

Among those named by Eaton as responding to the Williams proposal were Justin Winsor of the Boston Public Library, the foremost librarian of the country, William F. Poole of the Chicago Public Library, Henry A. Homes, of the New York State Library, and Lloyd P. Smith of the Library Company of Philadelphia. In his solicitation Commissioner Eaton had not overlooked the Librarian of Congress, A. R. Spofford, who did not "seem sanguine that a Convention of librarians would accomplish much practical good."[17]

Nothing really came of Williams' letter, despite the implication of the government report that he somehow had a direct connection with the preparations for the 1876 conference.[18] He did not attend the Philadelphia conference nor do letters exist indicating that he made suggestions about its program. However, he should be given credit for stimulating thought about a library conference in the months preceding the actual conference preparations. John Eaton himself suggested the logic of librarians meeting during the centennial, since other educational and scientific bodies would undoubtedly do the same.[19] Other extant letters also suggest that the idea of a library meeting was much in the air early in 1876, and some prominent librarians had already reacted favorably to such proposals.

According to traditional library history, the 1876 conference wheels were set in motion at a meeting in New York on May 17–18, 1876, in the offices of Frederick Leypoldt, editor and publisher of *Publishers' Weekly*.[20] Leypoldt, an indefatigable promoter of bibliographical work, had begun publishing notes on libraries in the first number of his journal in 1872, had published a special "Library Number" in October of the same year, and in January, 1876, had begun a regular department called "Library and Bibliographical Notes." An idealist infected with the same sort of enthusiasm as Dewey, Leypoldt saw libraries as important agencies in book distribution. In his perusal of foreign journals, he had noted the suggestion of an anonymous correspondent of the London *Academy*, for March 18, 1876, that an international congress of librarians would be very productive. Almost a month later, in the April 22 issue of *Publishers' Weekly*, Leypoldt published the *Academy* letter in its entirety. At the same time the Boston Athenæum librarian, Charles Ammi Cutter, noted the suggestion with approval in the April 20 issue of *The Nation*.

During late April and early May, Leypoldt and his partner, Richard Rodgers Bowker, apparently discussed various methods of library cooperation and Bowker turned his attention to writing an editorial on the subject for the May 20 issue of *Publishers' Weekly*. Just as the issue was about ready to go to press, Melvil Dewey, "a library enthusiast from the Amherst College Library," to use Leypoldt's phrase, appeared in New York to discuss his proposed *American Library Journal*. Since he had already entertained the thought of establishing a separate library periodical, Leypoldt immediately became interested in the new journal which Dewey had already planned with the Ginn brothers of Boston. He and Bowker discussed with Dewey how they could merge their interests in such an undertaking. Leypoldt told Dewey that they had been preparing an editorial urging a library conference for their library number, which was now ready for the press. Dewey heartily seconded the idea of a conference and said he had already talked with Justin Winsor and other Boston librarians concerning such cooperation. He thought they would be happy to assist.[21]

Somewhat peculiarly in view of Dewey's later assertions that he had been thinking about a library conference for from one to three years, there is no evidence in the transcription of the Dewey diaries from January 1, 1875, through June 11, 1876, indicating any concern with such a conference before this May 17 meeting with Bowker and Leypoldt. Admittedly this is an argument from silence, though one wonders why, if the conference idea were such a major part of Dewey's thinking, it was absent from his record of personal activities. Certainly other

8

Dewey proposals such as metric reform, simplified spelling, the library journal, and classification, all received attention. Dewey did hold numerous discussions with Boston librarians in April and May, 1876, and the conference idea may have been included in their conversations. The question which has to be asked is whether or not the idea was expressed in more than general terms prior to the meeting with Bowker and Leypoldt. I personally think not. Bowker later stated that the conference idea came partly from the 1853 Conference and partly from the favorable response to the recently formed American Book Trade Association in which Leypoldt was actively engaged. The editorial in the first issue of the *American Library Journal* also gives credit for the conference idea to the May meeting and the 1853 Conference. Since this is the document closest to the actual date, its statement should be given the highest consideration.

Neither Leypoldt nor Bowker has received as much credit for the origin of the Conference as they are due. They were essentially modest men, who provided the quiet background support necessary for the success of any new venture, while Dewey was never reluctant to claim his full share of the credit for 1876. The only point which would bring Bowker charging to the defense was the thought that the *Library Journal* was the product of the Conference and the Association. As he so rightly insisted, it was the other way around. Neither was he willing to give Dewey all the credit for the *Journal*, which he maintained was an older idea discussed by him and Leypoldt. When Bowker was having difficulty with Dewey over the publication of the *Library Journal* a year and a half later, he wrote Cutter, "As to ed. relations, I have opposed not at all his equality but the supremacy he claims, on the ground that D. alone originated the *Journal*. He deserves full credit for the Conf., the Conv. the splendid advances made in library arrangements—much, but not *all*, for the *Journal*, wh. was an old idea of Mr. L. and myself, too."[22] If Bowker felt especially sensitive on this point, he had a right to be; Bowker and Leypoldt insured the *Library Journal's* success by subsidizing its deficits for the first ten years of its existence. Still, his courtesy was always apparent, even when he felt he must disagree; and he was frequently willing to forego his own share of the credit.

Except for the massive Bureau of Education report, which cites Williams' letter, all subsequent published literature refers to this May 17–18 meeting as the beginning step in the formation of the American Library Association. In a very real sense this is true, although it is not

9

the whole story. In addition to the background already described above, there were other significant influences which played their part.

Having decided to join forces, the three individuals, two from the book trade and one from the library world, drew up the proof of a call for a library conference which they sent to several eastern librarians, while telegrams were dispatched to W. F. Poole at Chicago, Charles Evans at Indianapolis, and Thomas Vickers at Cincinnati.[23] This preliminary document asked approval of various chief librarians for the calling of a meeting in Philadelphia on August 15, 1876, or on such other date as might be generally acceptable. This "proof" was signed by Leypoldt, Dewey, W. I. Fletcher of the Watkinson Library (unauthorized), and L. E. Jones.

On May 19, Dewey journeyed to Philadelphia, where he saw Commissioner of Education John Eaton, who agreed to participate in the venture and placed the facilities of the Bureau at Dewey's disposal in sending out the official call. Strong initial reaction to such a document might well have been anticipated. There were many librarians who were immediately enthusiastic. Among these were the youngsters such as Charles Evans at Indianapolis (then 25) and William T. Peoples of the New York Mercantile Library (then 33), although one of the oldest, Lloyd P. Smith of Philadelphia, came quickly into the camp.

Yet the response of the library leaders, those with influence and power, could at best be described as lukewarm. Justin Winsor, later to be president of the American Library Association for its first ten years, noted that he was willing to do anything helpful for the library cause; but he did not think that he could make it to Philadelphia in a centennial August. Spofford's attitude as Librarian of Congress has already been made clear; and Poole, who had never heard of Dewey, wrote Winsor, "It won't pay for you and me to attend that barbecue."[24] In short, the real leaders were not going to be hoodwinked by a wild-eyed young radical and a couple of tradesmen from the publishers' association.

Youth and age have traditionally been at odds with each other, and the library profession is no exception. In a report on the second library conference held in New York City in 1877, *The World* (New York), published the following:

> As in all conventions, a slight division is apparent. The party of young librarians was eager for the adoption of Continental methods, for decapitalization in the French style, and uniformity of labels, in-

dexes and calendars, to which the conservative majority gave guarded encouragement. To hear the frank, mirthful Dewey, editor of the *Librarian's Monthly* [sic] or the earnest, enthusiastic young Tyler, who has stepped from the Astor Library to the head of the rich and growing Johns Hopkins at Baltimore, enlarging on the advantages of omitting all capitals possible in a catalogue of books, one was fain to look upon it as a chief earthly interest, while the emphatic Spofford, who has charge of the Congressional Library, or the deprecatory Homes of Albany, and Poole of Chicago protest against any such neo republicanism of letters and beheading of capitals.[25]

That this situation had also occurred a year earlier was confirmed by William E. Foster, next to Dewey the youngest man at the 1876 Conference. According to Foster the spirit of innovation was not generally acceptable in 1876, and the librarians in convention assembled were certainly not the vanguard.[26]

It was as obvious to Dewey as to anyone else that support from the leaders was essential; but it was equally clear, later, that the conference would not have succeeded without Dewey's youth, energy, and enthusiasm, a fact which Winsor, Poole, and Cutter all acknowledged publicly.[27]

Since Poole subsequently fought Dewey's proposals on a number of occasions, there has arisen the pleasant fiction that Poole was the strongest and possibly the only strong opponent of the convention idea. Such a conception may not be unrelated to Poole's argumentative nature and his vigor in debate on controversial issues. He and Dewey were alike in the certainty that their own view of a problem was the the right view. While it is true that Poole was leery of endorsing a conference whose originators he did not know, his opposition has been much overstressed, as his biographer, W. L. Williamson, has pointed out.[28] Not only was he joined by others in the sentiment that librarians should not proceed blindly on such matters, but his postcard of May 31, to Winsor, may well have saved the day for the conference and the association. Poole insisted that he would not sign an official call unless Winsor personally started the whole business anew and promised to attend. His ultimatum had its effect. Once Winsor so promised, Poole sailed into the fray and became one of the most valuable members of the conference planning committee. Years after Poole's death, even while acknowledging his contribution, Dewey related that Poole had a feeling "the movement had one foot in the grave and the other foot on a banana peel."[29] The statement is much too strong. Although Poole did not hesitate to be blunt in his letters, his advice was usually worth heeding; and, once convinced, he was sincerely interested in making the conference a success.[30]

By mid-June enough of the leading librarians had signed the call to warrant its printing and general distribution. Among those who signed were Justin Winsor, Charles Ammi Cutter, John Langdon Sibley of Harvard, S. F. Haven of the American Antiquarian Society, Addison VanName of Yale, Lloyd P. Smith, Henry A. Homes of the New York State Library, and, of course, Poole and Dewey. Leypoldt and L. E. Jones discreetly left their names off the list; and Fletcher's was not included because his boss, J. H. Trumbull, was opposed to the whole idea.[31] This first printed call was forwarded to librarians all over the country, and their responses immediately began to come into the New York office of *Publishers' Weekly*.

Librarians from all types of libraries—private, society, law, medical, theological, free public, the large and the small, and the geographically dispersed—responded to the initial call. Some of the best suggestions came from librarians of the smaller libraries who had looked to the Boston Public Library's *Bulletin* or to correspondence with the major librarians for their guidance. Indicative of the status of these libraries is the fact that they had to contain only 300 volumes to be listed in the government report. Mrs. Emily F. Carnes of Galveston, Texas, of whom practically nothing is known, gave an excellent overview of the problems of the small library. As librarian in a small community (albeit an important one in its region), she was not only isolated from the mainstream of library development but had to battle against the natural inertia of the public. She was not alone. There are other names, such as that of Mrs. H. L. Patterson, librarian of the year-old Muncie, Ind., Public Library, who felt it essential that she attend the conference, but somehow did not make it. Daniel W. Fink, State Law Librarian of Rhode Island, was disappointed that he did not see the names of more law librarians on the printed call, since he thought that they needed cooperation as much as any other group. One wonders if this isn't still true of this group of separatists.

These librarians wanted many topics discussed, but they especially wanted to know what to do about cataloging and classification, indexing magazines, creating other bibliographical tools, and the mutilation and pilfering of library materials. Classification was far from narrowing down to two basic schemes nor was there anything like general agreement on cataloging rules. With free public libraries springing up all over the country and with academic libraries soon to receive the full impact of the Germanic research emphasis, no topics were to receive more time, thought, and discussion than the classification system or the cataloging rules to be adopted. Both Dewey's classification and Cutter's rules, which appeared later that year,[32] were seminal publications with far-reaching impact upon the profession. Time and again in their plans to attend the conference, the letter writers also urged that the proceedings be published. Those who sent regrets were especially eager to see the data they hoped would be forthcoming.

Soon a conference planning committee was formed with Justin Winsor as chairman, assisted by Lloyd P. Smith and William F. Poole, with Melvil Dewey serving as Conference Secretary. The reason for Poole's insistence upon Winsor as chairman is not difficult to reconstruct. He was unquestionably the leading American librarian in 1876. The vigorous growth of the Boston Public Library and its innovations in library methodology provided inspiration for struggling librarians in less favored circumstances. Moreover, Winsor's scholarly mind thoroughly investigated every situation before he formulated his own principles. His annual reports, with their mass of comparative data on libraries abroad as well as those in America, foreshadowed the report from the Bureau of Education. Indeed when John Eaton decided to investigate the library situation in the country he turned to Winsor for advice and the final product owed much to Winsor's suggestions. Libraries as far away as Tokyo sought his annual reports and bulletins.[33] Winsor was frequently consulted by new library boards. Hence, his name on the conference call was an assurance to most librarians that such a conference would be well worth attending.

In 1876 Winsor was in the prime of life (age 45); a man of dignity and mild manners, he seemed destined to preside over scholarly meetings.[34] When he spoke, his low-pitched voice carried to all corners of the room, and nothing escaped his tireless eyes. Meetings over which he presided were always under complete control. He and Poole were long-time friends and frequently in agreement on the main points at issue. They were *conservatives*, in the best sense of that term, respecting rules but not fearing them. Both had broad knowledge of the management of all types of libraries, but they preferred their own solutions to problems in a given situation and cared little for a rigid conformity among

13

libraries. In his presidential address of 1879, Winsor clearly enunciated the dangers of cooperation as well as its virtues.[35] Although he was not so argumentative as his older colleague, Poole, he was not a stuffy man either. A subtle sense of humor is revealed in his "A Word to Starters of Libraries," in the first issue of the *American Library Journal* as well as in some of his other writings.[36] Winsor's was a steadying influence and he was always able to maintain a sense of balance in discussions; the fledgling association was fortunate to have him to steer its course for the first ten years.

The local chairman of the committee, Lloyd Pearsall Smith, had followed his father as librarian of the Library Company of Philadelphia. Smith was, as Poole said, "a conservative, and he had a right to be one,"[37] for he headed the oldest continuing library not connected with a college in the country. Since he was a Philadelphia resident and a member of the 1853 Conference, he was the obvious choice for local arrangements. Charles Evans noted that he was "jolly, companionable, and *at home.*"[38] Witty and gracious, Smith impressed all who came into contact with him by his charm. Another member of the conference said of Smith: "His cordial greetings, his kindly interest in everybody and his natural politeness in listening quietly and amiably to all views expressed, including those which his conservative nature and education could not approve, made him a very valuable member of the conference and the Association."[39]

In a period of rapidly expanding public libraries, heavily used by the people, Smith reportedly never accepted their necessity. Dewey related that he had once visited Smith in the recently completed Ridgway Branch in Philadelphia. Expecting to see two or three hundred people, he was surprised to see only three or four and asked Smith if this were the average attendance. Smith responded, "Dewey, there is scarcely a day that *somebody* doesn't come into this library."[40]

Of Poole, perhaps enough has been said to indicate that he was a giant of a man, both physically and mentally. A towering six-footer, like Winsor he wore a beard; but unlike Winsor he had side whiskers which gave him the appearance of the "old rat," an expression Dewey facetiously used to describe him to Bowker.[41] His gruff, Western manner made him a vigorous opponent in debate, and "plain talk" was his trade-mark.

However, his exterior concealed a kindly spirit; and his genius for friendship among his subordinates made them loyal to him for life.

When he read a paper, he had a most benignant manner, and he would pause occasionally to ad lib with the impression of taking the audience into his confidence. Poole had successively been librarian of the Boston Mercantile, Boston Athenæum, Cincinnati Public, and the Chicago Public libraries. He had trained many apprentices who worked in libraries throughout the country and his periodical index was widely known and appreciated. As Dewey said of him, perhaps in a calculating manner but nonetheless truly, "We can't do without you and feel satisfied. Your name is always mentioned among the very first, and it would look all wrong not to see it in the list we now have."[42]

Few librarians have ever been neutral about the Conference Secretary, Melvil Dewey. The man arouses the strongest emotions pro and con. In the late nineteenth century he had numerous disciples who went forth to spread the missionary word about "securing the best reading for the largest number at the least expense."[43] Through his subsequent editorship of the *Library Journal* and his position as Secretary of the American Library Association, Dewey soon became known as the foremost exponent of modern librarianship. Many of his ideas were subsequently accepted unquestioningly by his disciples. He also aroused annoyance, and sometimes antagonism, among a smaller number. One of Poole's protégés described the uncritical proponents of Dewey's methods as "Dewey-worshippers," while another noted that he had "been so long on the Publishing Board with Mr. Dewey that I have got thoroughly in the habit, when he gets through, of saying something on the other side . . . ."[44] Dewey's son has stated that his father was rarely without a harrassing number of enemies, partly because of his business integrity, but more probably from his occasional failures in tact and patience.[45]

Because of hero-worship, Dewey's position has been somewhat obscured "as it was in the beginning." At the time of the conference Dewey was not quite 25 and apparently the youngest conference member. Like Poole, he was a six-footer, but with a wiry, loose-knit frame and no beard—only sideburns.[46] Alert on his feet, he had a head full of ideas which poured forth rapidly in a high-pitched voice. He had come to Boston, the acknowledged "hub" of the library world, to found a library periodical, a metric bureau, and an organization to reform spelling, all at the same time. Along with this tremendous energy, there was a streak of stubbornness in Dewey; and, if he found his way blocked in one direction, he merely achieved his goal by going another route.

He had a strong sense of his own righteousness and could be irritatingly prudish about smoking and other vices of which he disapproved. At the conference during a committee meeting, Smith and Poole stepped out for a smoke. Dewey took the opportunity to ram through his proposals. When Poole subsequently protested the final report, Dewey noted it had been voted on when a minority retired "shall I say it—to smoke."[47]

Yet Dewey's skill and persistence in the office of Conference Secretary represented major contributions to its success. Most of the detailed work of the meeting preparations fell on him; and he performed them well, jotting down his shorthand notes on letters, sending items off to Winsor for concurrence, and prodding the conference committee for decisions. Nor can one fault Dewey on his bold conceptions and his creative vision. With the metric system, spelling reform, and a library conference and journal all teeming in his brain at the same time, only an essentially likeable young man could have succeeded in arousing so little antagonism among the naturally conservative leaders of the emerging profession.

Writing to Bowker after the conference, Poole commented, "It is cruel to put so much work upon one person, even if he is a good fellow. Dewey is a remarkable man, and I have become much interested in him."[48] When they had first met at Lloyd P. Smith's house prior to the conference, Poole had come across the parlor, drawn himself up to his full height, and said laughingly, "Well, Dewey, you are a better looking man than I thought you were."[49] As Foster perceptively notes, "both by correspondence and by personal interviews and appeals he succeeded in overcoming the natural inertia of the men most influential in this connection, and in bringing together a representative gathering in October."[50] Despite some exaggerated claims about the conference origin, Melvil Dewey deserves full credit for bringing to fruition an idea which had not gone beyond the discussion stage among his colleagues.

In line with various suggestions, the conference committee changed the date from August 15 to October 4–6 to take advantage of the cooler weather. They accepted an offer from the Historical Society of Pennsylvania to provide meeting rooms without charge. In late July the U. S. Bureau of Education mailed a second printed circular, giving the new date and place of meeting. Some 2,000 copies were sent to librarians in this country and abroad. Meanwhile, Dewey was writing prospective speakers; and, in mid-September, he distributed the program in the form of advance proofs from the first number of the *American*

Library Journal. He urged the centennial exhibition as an added attraction for librarians from a distance to make the effort to go to Philadelphia.

The rest is history, and that fairly well reported. On Wednesday morning, October 4, 1876, the Librarians' Conference opened in the halls of the Historical Society of Pennsylvania. The society's president, John William Wallace, gave the opening address; and behind him, seated in a semicircular recess of a bay window, sat the librarians of Philadelphia. Wallace's speech of welcome summarized well the major problems confronting librarians of the day: the need to cope bibliographically with the flood of books, the kind of building to erect, the kind of classification and the direction of the printed catalog, specialized collections, and the need for developing a new science—"BIBLIO-THECAL SCIENCE." The conference then proceeded to organize itself, promptly electing Justin Winsor president, and A. R. Spofford, James Yates, William F. Poole, and Lloyd P. Smith vice-presidents. Winsor moved quickly to the appointment of committees and the organization of the conference. Dewey, Evans, and Guild were elected secretaries, an especially important election since Poole had refused to let Dewey hire a stenographer because of the expense.[51] Dewey then asked every librarian to register and reported that he had received a telegram from Samuel R. Warren of the Bureau of Education stating that he had started from Washington for the conference with copies of the government report.

The initial organization took most of the morning; but when the conference reassembled at 3 p.m., it began a furious pace which "horrified the reporters" and later horrified the secretaries, who had to prepare the proceedings for issuance as a double number of the *American Library Journal*.

Dewey called attention to the burden this put upon the secretaries in his report: "The absence of a stenographer encouraged freedom of debate, but it put upon the secretaries and editors a Herculean task in the after-gathering of the *disjecta membra*. Most of the speakers have been furnished with a minute of the details in which they took part, and requested to write out their remarks; the results have been worked, revised, and reworked into shape, in consultation with several officers. This method approximates accuracy, but it has caused great delay . . . ." That the secretaries were highly successful is apparent from "The Proceedings."[52] Eleven formal papers were delivered, beginning with that of Poole on "Some Popular Objections to Libraries." Following each paper there was lengthy discussion which called forth diverse opinions as well as the testimony of personal experience.

Of the 103 who registered, 90 were men and 13 were women, a ratio of the sexes which was later almost to reverse itself. Seventeen states were represented, although the largest attendance was from the East Coast, with the South not being represented at all. Among the non-librarians present were Dr. Daniel Read, retired president of the University of Missouri, and Henry Barnard, educator, of Hartford, Connecticut. Although most of the leading librarians were there, several distinguished names were missing. None of the Harvard librarians attended, nor did anyone from St. Louis. Both Haven of the American Antiquarian Society and John Shaw Billings of the Surgeon-General's Library could not be present but they did send personal representatives.

There were a variety of libraries represented, including 13 from academic libraries, 43 from private, subscription or special libraries, and 24 from free public libraries.[53] However, even though the public librarians were in the minority, it was they who controlled the convention and who notably advanced the Association which came out of it. Moreover, as Boromé has pointed out, while there were conservatives and liberals, visionaries and standpatters, the librarians at Philadelphia were "positive individuals who had entered upon their calling by choice."[54] They were not school teachers who couldn't teach, lawyers incapable of practicing, nor clergymen whose only merit was "that bronchitis was a demerit in their original calling."[55] In short, they were professionals, with a strong sense of professional responsibility, who wanted their place in the educational sun.

One cannot resist noting that—whether the profession has advanced so little in the past 90 years or whether basic problems tend to persist from generation to generation—the Association is still debating some of the same issues raised by the conference. Indeed, the beginning librarian might well be given the excellent address of John William Wallace as an admirable summary of contemporary problems. Perhaps it is true that the more things change the more they remain the same.

On the third day of the conference came the call to form a permanent organization. All of those who wanted to join the new Association were urged to sign the register. The irrepressible Dewey, with characteristic flourish, took the book and wrote, "Number one, Melvil Dewey."[56] He then passed it to Charles Evans who signed as number two. Before the end of the year a total of 41 persons had joined the fledgling Association. The following year saw the membership rise to 110, and by the end of 1878 it had reached 197.[57] Although it was at least a decade before the Association could be said to be on a sound footing, the profession never lost that initial momentum. Unlike the 1853 conference, the Library Conference of 1876 really sparked a movement.

According to the latest report, membership in the American Library Association reached 34,754 at the end of 1966. As Mr. Dewey prophesied so well in the *American Library Journal:*

> Of the permanent results of the Conference, the organization of the American Library Association must be put first, because this means the frequent repetition of the Conference; a recognized authority which may promote or endorse desirable improvements, and furnish decisions on the many points at issue in which prospective general usage is the sufficient criterion; and otherwise a chance to reap the benefits of organized co-operation.[58]

NOTES

[1]*Allan Nevins*, The Emerging of Modern America, 1865-1876 (*"History of American Life," Vol. VIII*), (*New York: Macmillan, 1927*), *ch. xi, "Two Memorable Years: 1873 and 1876," esp. p. 317.*

[2]*The phrases come from the first and second printed calls. See items 29 and 62.*

[3]*As quoted by Dewey, "The American Library Association,"* ALJ, *1(March 31, 1877),* [245]-246. *The first volume was called* American Library Journal, *but at the end of the year "American" was dropped from the title to reflect its international scope.*

[4]*Henry R. Tedder, "Introduction," p.* [ix] *and John Winter Jones, "Inaugural Address," p.* [1], *Conference of Librarians, London, 1877,* Transactions and Proceedings (*London: Chiswick Press, 1878*).

[5]*U.S. Department of the Interior, Bureau of Education,* Public Libraries in the United States of America; Their History, Condition, and Management, *Special Report, pts. 1 and 2 (Washington: Government Printing Office, 1876), cited hereafter as* Public Libraries in the U. S., *1876.*

[6]*Richard R. Bowker, "Seed Time and Harvest—The Story of the A.L.A.,"* A.L.A. Bulletin, *20 (Oct., 1926), 304.*

[7]*Spofford to Leypoldt, ALS, May 29, 1876.*

[8]Ibid.

[9]*Dewey, "Past, Present, and Future of the A.L.A.," LJ, 5 (Sept.-Oct., 1880), 274.*

[10]*George B. Utley,* The Librarian's Conference of 1853; A Chapter in American Library History (*Chicago: American Library Association, 1951*), *pp. 10-15.*

[11]Ibid., *pp. 131-132, reproduces the printed call.*

[12]*Poole, "Address of the President," LJ, 11 (July, 1886), 199-200.*

[13]*Utley,* op. cit., *pp. 84, 99-101.*

[14]*Arthur M. Schlesinger,* The Rise of the City, 1878-1898 (*"A History of American Life," Vol. X*), (*New York: Macmillan, 1933*), ch. vii, "Increasing the World's Knowledge," *esp. pp. 220-222. Arthur E. Bestor, Jr., "The Transformation of American Scholarship, 1875-1917," Library Quarterly, 23 (July, 1953), 173-174.*

[15]*Bowker, "A Postscript," LJ, 21 (Feb., 1896), 52. For Dewey's later comments see Dewey, "What the A.L.A. Was Meant to Be and to Do,"* Wisconsin Library Bulletin, *13 (Feb., 1917), 41-42.*

[16]*Williams to Eaton, copy of letter dated incorrectly Aug. 3, 1876, Minneapolis Athenæum. Eaton to Williams, Lbk, Feb. 7, 1876, National Archives.*

[17]*Eaton to Williams, Lbk, Feb. 7, 1876, National Archives.*

[18]Public Libraries in the U. S., *1876, p. xxvii.*

[19]*Eaton to Winsor, LS, July 2, 1875, Superintendent's File, BPL.*

[20]*This fairly standard story can be found in numerous articles by Bowker and is well summarized in Jay W. Beswick,* The Work of Frederick Leypoldt, Bibliographer and Publisher (*New York: R.R. Bowker Co., 1942*), *pp. 51-58. See also Frederic M. Melcher, "Among the Founders," LJ, 76 (Dec. 1, 1951), 1960; and E. McClung Fleming,* R. R. Bowker: Militant Liberal (*Norman: University of Oklahoma Press, 1952*), *pp. 57-58.*

[21]*Dewey, "Dairy," no. 5, May 18, 1876, Dewey Papers, CUL.*

[22]*Bowker to Cutter, Lbk, Jan. 3, 1878, Bowker Papers, NYPL.*

[23]*Bowker stated that he wrote the circular letter and the telegrams sent to the leading librarians. Bowker, "The Library Journal and Library Organization: A Twenty Years' Retrospect," LJ, 21 (Jan., 1896), 5.*

[24]*Poole to Winsor, postcard, signed, May 31, 1876, Superintendent's File,* BPL.

[25]*"The Librarians' Convention,"* The World (*New York*), *Sept. 7, 1877, p. 5, col. 1.*

²⁶*Foster, "Five Men of '76,"* A.L.A. Bulletin, *20 (Oct., 1926), 320.*

²⁷*Winsor, "The President's Address,"* LJ, *2 (Sept., 1877), 6; Poole, "Address of the President,"* LJ, *11 (July, 1886), 201; Cutter "Cooperation Committee,"* LJ, *4 (July-Aug., 1879), 287.*

²⁸*William L. Williamson,* William Frederick Poole and the Modern Library Movement *("Columbia University Studies in Library Service," no. 13), (New York: Columbia University Press, 1963), ch. vii.*

²⁹*Dewey, "Our Next Half-Century,"* A.L.A. Bulletin, *20 (Oct., 1926), 309-310.*

³⁰*Poole's own defense is summed up in his letter to Dewey, ALS, Dec. 28, 1883, Dewey Papers, CUL.*

³¹*Poole to Winsor, ALS, Sept. 18, 1876, Superintendent's File, BPL.*

³²*[Dewey],* A Classification and Subject Index for Cataloguing and Arranging the Books and Pamphlets of a Library *(Amherst, Mass., 1876), 42 pp. Dewey's preface is dated June 10, 1876. Charles Ammi Cutter,* Rules for a Printed Dictionary Catalogue *(Washington: Government Printing Office, 1876), 89 pp., pt. II of* Public Libraries in the U. S., *1876.*

³³*Joseph A. Boromé, "The Life and Letters of Justin Winsor," (Unpublished Ph.D. dissertation, Columbia University, 1950), pp. 218-224.*

³⁴*Description of Winsor is from Boromé, "Life and Letters of Justin Winsor," passim; Foster, "Five Men of '76,"* A.L.A. Bulletin, *20 (Oct., 1926), 313-314; Samuel Swett Green,* The Public Library Movement in the United States, *1853-1893 . . . (Boston: The Boston Book Company, 1913), pp. 25-30; and "The Librarian's Convention,"* The World *(New York), Sept. 7, 1877, p. 5, col. 1.*

³⁵*Winsor, "The President's Address,"* LJ, *2 (Sept., 1877), [5]-7.*

³⁶*Winsor, "A Word to Starters of Libraries,"* ALJ, *1 (Sept. 30, 1876), 1-3.*

³⁷*Poole, "Address of the President,"* LJ, *11 (July, 1886), 204.*

³⁸*Evans to Dewey, postcard, signed, June 24, 1876.*

³⁹*Green,* Public Library Movement, *p. 39. The description of Smith is largely from Green's book.*

⁴⁰*Dewey, "Our Next Half-Century,"* A.L.A. Bulletin, *20 (Oct., 1926), 309.*

⁴¹*Dewey to Bowker, LS, Oct. 24, 1876, Bowker Papers, NYPL. The description of Poole is from Williamson,* William Frederick Poole, *passim; Green,* Public Library Movement, *pp. 30-34; his letters and the early proceedings of the American Library Association.*

[42]*Dewey to Poole, June 5, 1876, as quoted in Poole to Dewey, ALS, Dec. 28, 1883, Dewey Papers, CUL.*

[43]*Dewey, "The American Library Association," ALJ, 1 (March 31, 1877), 247.*

[44]*Mary Abbie Bean to Charles Evans, ALS, Aug. 10, 1890, Evans Papers, IUL. W.I. Fletcher, "Proceedings," LJ, 26 (1901), c139.*

[45]*Godfrey Dewey, "Dewey, 1851-1951," LJ, 76 (Dec. 1, 1951), 1964.*

[46]*Description of Dewey from a variety of sources including Foster, "Five Men of '76," A.L.A. Bulletin, 20 (Oct., 1926), 318-320; Fremont Rider, Melvil Dewey (Chicago: A.L.A., 1944), passim, as well as his diaries, letters, and published materials in the early LJ.*

[47]*ALJ, 1 (Nov. 30, 1876), 140.*

[48]*Poole to Bowker, ALS, Nov. 14, 1876, Bowker Papers, NYPL.*

[49]*Dewey at the Lake Placid Conference, LJ, 19 (Dec., 1894), 170.*

[50]*Foster, "Five Men of '76," A.L.A. Bulletin, 20 (Oct., 1926), 319.*

[51]*Poole to Dewey, postcard, signed, Sept. 18, 1876.*

[52]"The Proceedings," *ALJ, 1 (Nov. 30, 1876), 91-145.*

[53]*Williamson, "William Frederick Poole and the Modern Library Movement," (Unpublished dissertation, University of Chicago, 1959), pp. 363-365, is the source of this analysis.*

[54]*Boromé, "Life and Letters of Justin Winsor," p. 241.*

[55]*Winsor, "Free Libraries and Readers," ALJ, 1 (Nov. 30, 1876), 67.*

[56]*William Stetson Merrill, "Early Days at the Newberry Library: Reminiscences of Persons and Events, 1889 to 1894," typewritten MS, Oconomowoc, Wis., March 15, 1954, p. 23 verso, in Newberry Library, Chicago.*

[57]*American Library Association, "Membership List, Including Register of Members Present at Boston and Other Conferences," printed list bound with LJ, 4 (1879), but probably published separately.*

[58][Dewey, "Editorial"], *ALJ, 1 (Nov. 30, 1876), 90-91.*

1. LONDON ACADEMY CORRESPONDENCE— A LIBRARY CONGRESS

A CORRESPONDENT writes:—

"In these days of International Congresses, it is strange that no attempt should have been made to convene a Congress of Librarians. Very great improvements have of late years been made in the arrangement and management of public and private libraries. In some the machinery for placing and shifting books, in others the binding, in others again the classifying and cataloguing of books have been brought to great perfection; but though there are journals in which these improvements, and what may in some cases be added, these new discoveries, are discussed, there has seldom been, what is so useful, an exchange of ideas by word of mouth between those who know the real difficulties that have to be met, and the success that has attended recent experiments. Let me mention one point only.

"When I was a librarian myself, I always wondered at the extraordinary waste of power in cataloguing new books. While I was writing my slip, according to the rules followed in most English libraries, I felt that there were probably a hundred people doing exactly the same work which I was doing, not only in England, but in every civilised country of the world. Yet what would be easier than to have my slip printed, and any number of copies sent round by book-post to every library in Europe? With a little arrangement, every English book might be catalogued at the British Museum, every French book at the Bibliothèque Nationale, every German book at the Royal Library at Berlin, every Russian book at St. Petersburg, &c. At a trifling expense these printed slips might be sent to every small or large library, and each of them might have three or four kinds of catalogues—an alphabetical catalogue of the authors, a chronological catalogue, a local catalogue, a catalogue classified according to subjects, &c. Even when a library is too poor to buy a book, the slip might be useful in its catalogue. The saving that might thus be effected would be very considerable. The staff of librarians might be greatly reduced, and the enormous expense now incurred for catalogues, and mostly imperfect catalogues, would dwindle down to a mere nothing.

"There are, of course, other ways in which the same object might be obtained, if only the principal libraries would agree on a common line of action. Each author might be requested to write a proper slip of his own

23

book, and the publisher might forward copies of these slips with the book itself.

"All this and much more could be done, if a general understanding was once arrived at between the librarians of the principal libraries of Europe. If we look at the balance-sheets of these libraries, the differences are very great. The expenses are, of course, much greater where books are lent out, than where they are not. But even where the expenses are lowest, the chief item of expenditure is always the catalogue. A few resolutions, carried at an International Congress of Librarians, might cause a saving of many thousands of pounds annually, and would certainly give us better catalogues than we find at present even in best administered libraries."

Anonymous writer in *The Academy* (London), March 18, 1876, pp. 261-262. This item was noticed by Frederick Leypoldt and reprinted in *PW*, 9 (April 22, 1876), 528. It was probably Charles A. Cutter (1837–1903), Librarian, Boston Athenæum, 1868–1893, who noted the same suggestion in *The Nation*, 22 (April 20, 1876), 264, where he commented that the scheme for a catalog by the national library had been set forth in the *Tribune* nearly a year before.[1] He added, "A Congress of Librarians in the United States could be called any time, and perhaps never more appropriately than during the present year." During the month of April, 1876, Dewey saw Cutter frequently, and it is entirely possible that they could have discussed this proposal, although Dewey makes no mention of such a discussion in his diary.

[1]*Cutter is known to have written two articles in* The Nation *on the library conference, and it seems probable that he wrote the other short notes as well. Daniel C. Haskell, comp.,* The Nation, *Volumes 1-105 . . . Indexes of Titles and Contributors (New York: New York Public Library, 1953), II, iii-iv, 116.*

2. *MELVIL DEWEY'S DIARY*

MAY 17, 1876 [NEW YORK]

After breakfast at Frenches did an errand or so and then found Leypoldt in, and also Bowker. I talked with him about the journal, and he said at once that he was anxious to have a hand in the enterprise. He discussed the plan, etc., and I agreed, after a long talk, to come in in the morning and see what they had written for a library editorial . . . .

Excerpt from entry in Dewey, "Diary," no. 5, Dewey Papers, CUL. The transcriptions of the two diaries I have examined are no. 4, which has the typed heading "Lake Placid Club, Lake Placid, Florida, January, 1932" with the date "1 January 1875 to 10 April 1876," and, in someone's handwriting, "Biscoe Copy," and no. 5, headed simply "Melvil Dewey, April 10, 1876–June 11, 1876" with a handwritten addition "Aug., 1877." The transcription from Dewey's shorthand is rough and I have smoothed an occasional word or two. Dewey had started for New York from Boston on the evening of May 16, presumably a date he could later fix with accuracy. There is some confusion about what took place with respect to the library conference, since the diary states the conference idea was broached on the 18th, while the letter from Leypoldt and Dewey to Justin Winsor is clearly dated May 17 and Winsor's response is dated May 18. In his other writing in the diaries, Dewey indicates that he did not always write daily, but later summarized events. Did Bowker and Leypoldt send the letter to Winsor without Dewey's knowledge or before the conference idea had been rather thoroughly discussed? This seems unlikely. It is entirely probable that a letter to Winsor was first mailed (May 17) and on the following day letters and telegrams were dispatched to other librarians. I have not located any other letters or telegrams sent by Bowker. Dewey spent the rest of the day (May 17) on metric and publishing matters. That evening he attended a meeting of the American Metrological Society where he succeeded in having a committee appointed which would be favorably disposed to his ideas. In view of his activities on this busy day, he can be pardoned if the events of May 17 and 18 were a little unsettled when he later penned them. Unfortunately for this study, the diary ends with June 11, 1876, and does not resume until Aug. 27, 1877, where Dewey notes that it has been more than a year since he opened the book, but that the *Metric Bulletin, L.J., Spelling Reform Bulletin,* etc., will eventually aid him in "recovering the history of the eventful months just past." Since he wrote shorthand replies on many letters and urged Winsor to preserve them, he probably also expected the letters to help reconstruct his activities during June-October, 1876.

3. MELVIL DEWEY'S DIARY

MAY 18, 1876

Up and down town at about 8. Did not see Heath[1] .... Talked with Van Nostrand[2] about metric books .... Went over to Leypoldt and talked library matters until nearly 4 having dinner in the meantime with him and Bowker. We talked over the plans for the journal and the items on which we could unite interests. He said he wanted nothing to do with supplying blanks, books, etc., that I might furnish, using my position as director to help me in all such articles, only letting books alone which would run into the book trade. As he was unwilling to give up his plans for a library journal,[3] it seemed the only way to let him have it but I closed no bargain with him telling him I would write after talking with my 2 friends[4] who were in the project with me. He did not mistrust who they were. After a good deal of talk we decided it was best that I should stay in Boston, but the paper should be printed and distributed from N.Y. That he preferred to own it all and take his own risk. That I should receive for my services as editor $500 a year and 20% of gross receipts for subscriptions and advertising. That all my office and traveling expenses should be paid by him, that I should never work more than ½ time as an average, using this time when I thought best, resting myself when I thought best, etc., simply using my own judgment and counseling with him.[5] We then talked of trying for a library convention but were in trouble for the library number of [*Publishers' Weekly*] was just ready to print and the preliminary call must go in this. They said a number of prominent librarians wanted it and they had made the idea prominent in the paper then printing on that account. I told them that Fletcher of Hartford who was the most promising of the young librarians was in favor of such a convention and would surely sign the call as soon as it was offered to him, indeed from what he told me I should think it safe to put his name down on the list as in favor of the project. They said they would try and get some names for the paper and hold it a day or 2 ....

Excerpt from entry in Dewey, "Diary," no. 5, Dewey Papers, CUL.

[1]*Probably Daniel Collamore Heath (1843-1908), New York City representative of Ginn Brothers and subsequently a member of the firm.*

[2]*Probably David Van Nostrand (1811-1886), New York publisher.*

[3]*Both Winsor and Mrs. Leypoldt thought the journal would be a financial failure. Winsor felt that it would be better to have the library journal printed as a separate department of PW, an idea Dewey did not like. See Dewey, "Diary," no. 5, April 22, 1876. Mrs. Leypoldt later commented to Bowker, "I never believed in the Library Journal, because I knew it would not pay and I thought Dewey about as miserable a specimen of a gabbling idiot as I had ever beheld. Mr. L. was very angry with me because I would not see his argument that if he did not start the Journal, Dewey might carry his brilliant ideas somewhere else." A. H. Leypoldt to Bowker, ALS, Sept. 18, 1880, Bowker Papers, NYPL.*

[4]*Edwin and Fred Ginn of Ginn Brothers, Boston, with whom Dewey had already concluded an agreement on May 2, Dewey, "Diary," May 2, 1876.*

[5]*This agreement was to be the cause of great dissatisfaction between Dewey and Bowker in the years immediately following, and the dispute was not finally settled until 1887, long after Bowker had taken over the journal himself. "Statement as to 'Library Journal' and Melvil Dewey," 1887, TD, Dewey Papers, CUL. E. McClung Fleming, R. R. Bowker, pp. 61–66, is an excellent review of the problem.*

4. FREDERICK LEYPOLDT AND MELVIL DEWEY TO JUSTIN WINSOR

OFFICE OF THE PUBLISHERS' WEEKLY

New York, May 17, 1876

My dear Sir

We enclose herewith a preliminary call for a library conference, which we suppose will coincide with your views as expressed to Mr. Dewey. If so, will you kindly affix your signature and ask Mr. Perkins[1] and Mr. Whitney[2] to do the same?

Very Truly Yours
F. Leypoldt
Melvil Dewey
pk

AL. Superintendent's File, BPL. Frederick Leypoldt (1835–1884), publisher, bibliographer, founder and editor of *Publishers' Weekly*, 1872–1884. Melvil Dewey (1851–1931), Assistant Librarian, Amherst College Library, 1874–1876, and subsequently secretary of the American Library Association, 1876–1890. Justin Winsor (1831–1897), Superintendent, Boston Public Library, 1868–1877, and subsequently president of the American Library Association for the first ten years of its existence. Richard Rodgers Bowker (1848–1933), Leypoldt's associate, says that he wrote the circular letter (probably the preliminary call) and the telegrams sent out from the *PW* office. "The Library Journal and Library Organization: A Twenty Years' Retrospect," LJ, 21 (Jan., 1896), 5. Dewey apparently left the contacting of librarians for the project in the hands of Bowker and Leypoldt, and it seems probable that Bowker wrote and sent this letter too. See item 3.

¹*Frederic B. Perkins (1828-1899), Office Secretary and Assistant, Boston Public Library, 1874-1879.*

²*James Lyman Whitney (1835-1910), Assistant Superintendent and Head of the Catalog Department, Boston Public Library, 1874-1899. Whitney was associated with the Boston Public Library from 1869 until his death and was responsible for many of its printed catalogs and other publications.*

5. CALL FOR A LIBRARY CONFERENCE
(*PRELIMINARY "PROOF" CALL*)

DEAR SIR: The following call has been drawn up, at the suggestion of several leading librarians. If you approve of the plan, will you kindly affix your signature, and return at once to the office of the PUBLISHERS' WEEKLY, 37 Park Row?

> F. LEYPOLDT,
>
> MELVIL DEWEY,
> Amherst College Library.
>
> W. I. FLETCHER,[1]
> Watkinson Library, Hartford.
>
> E. L. Jones,[2]
> American Catalogue.

CALL FOR A LIBRARY CONFERENCE.

The undersigned, connected with the library interest of this country, believing that efficiency and economy in library work would be promoted by a conference of librarians which should afford opportunity for mutual consultation and practical co-operation, issue this preliminary call, inviting librarians and all interested in library work to meet at Philadelphia, on the 15th of August next, or at such other date as may be found more generally acceptable. A further call will be issued at a later date, and those intending to be present, and willing to sign such a call, are requested to send in their names, with suggestions as to topics to be presented, etc., to Melvil Dewey, care of the PUBLISHERS' WEEKLY, 37 Park Row, New York.

Printed Document. Superintendent's File, BPL. Included with letter of Leypoldt and Dewey to Winsor, May 17, 1876. This is undoubtedly the "circular letter" which Bowker stated that he wrote and sent to leading librarians in the East. Bowker, "The Library Journal and Library Organization : A Twenty Years' Retrospect," LJ, 21 (Jan., 1896), 5. On the right hand side of this copy of the document, opposite the names, is a manuscript note "printed by mistake." The meaning is uncertain but see footnote 1, below.

[1]*William Isaac Fletcher (1844–1917), Assistant Librarian, Watkinson Library, Hartford, Conn., 1874–1883. Was the note "printed by mistake" written because Fletcher objected to the unauthorized use of his name? Dewey had visited Fletcher in Hartford on May 11 and talked with him about a number of library matters. When Leypoldt brought up the subject of a library conference Dewey told him that Fletcher was one of the most promising of the younger librarians and they could go ahead and put his name down immediately (item 3). That Dewey misinterpreted the freedom with which he could use Fletcher's name is indicated by a subsequent diary entry where he notes that "Fletcher misunderstood the slip sent him & so we got into an awkward little hole. I telegraphed him as I took the boat for Boston . . ." (item 12). Fletcher's name does not appear on the two subsequent printed calls nor did he attend the convention. Poole said that Fletcher's superior, James Hammond Trumbull, was adamant that his library not be represented and wouldn't let Fletcher go (item 89). The result was that a librarian who had written extensively for the government report and who was to contribute significantly to the new association was not present at the organizational meeting.*

[2]*Lynds Eugene Jones (1853–1902), manager and compiler of the* American Catalogue, *under Leypoldt's direction.* Jones's name was transposed on the printed form.

29

6. THOMAS VICKERS TO LEYPOLDT

12:36 P.M.
Cincinnati, Ohio, May 18, 1876

You may add my name to call for a library conference.

Thos. Vickers

Telegram. Rev. Thomas Vickers (1835-1917), Librarian, Cincinnati Public Library, 1874-1879. Dewey's shorthand note on verso is difficult to transcribe, but probably reads: "Vickers Going to add call. Answer. 76/5/18."

7. CHARLES EVANS TO LEYPOLDT

Indianapolis, Ind., May 18, 1876

Excellent idea. Add my name and depend upon my attendance.

Charles Evans

Telegram. Charles Evans (1850-1935), first librarian, Indianapolis Public Library, 1872-1878, and subsequently the first treasurer of the Association, 1876-78.

8. *WINSOR AND J. L. WHITNEY TO LEYPOLDT*

BOSTON PUBLIC LIBRARY
Boston, May 18, 1876

My dear Sir,–

I am willing to do anything helpful for the cause of public library interests but my duties here and Philadelphia in a Centennial *August* will prevent, I think, personal participation. Mr. Perkins is in N.Y. and will probably see you before he returns. I will hand your slip & note to Mr. Whitney.

Very truly
Justin Winsor

Mr. Winsor has expressed my views. It is doubtful whether I can go to Philadelphia in August, as my work keeps me closely here.

J. L. Whitney

ALS. This is the first letter in the 1876 scrapbook and an answer to Leypoldt and Dewey's letter of May 17. Dewey's shorthand note: "Winsor and Whitney about call. Answer. 76/5/19."

First Entry in the Scrapbook

SUPERINTENDENT'S OFFICE.

(Central Department, Boylston St.)

JUSTIN WINSOR, Supt.
JAMES L. WHITNEY, Ass't Supt.
FREDERIC B. PERKINS, Office Sec.
CHARLES A. WILSON, Despatch Clerk.

BOSTON, ... May 15 ...... 1876.

My dear Sir,—

I am willing to do any-
thing helpful for the cause
of general library interests,
but my duties here and
Philadelphia in a
Centennial August will
prevent I think per-
sonal participation.
Mr. Perkins is in N.Y.

and will probably see
you before he returns.
I will have your
slip & note to Mr.
Whitney.

Very truly

Justin Winsor.

F. Reynolds Eq
37 Park Row
N.Y.

Mr. Winsor has expressed my views. It
is doubtful whether I can go to Philadelphia
in August, as my work keeps me closely here.

W.D. Whitney

9. WILLIAM F. POOLE TO WINSOR

PUBLIC LIBRARY OF CHICAGO
Chicago, May 18, 1876

My dear Winsor

I had a telegram[1] today from a party in New York whom I did not know asking if I would allow "us to add your signature to call for library conference at Phil. in August."

Do you know what this means, and whether such a conference has been agreed upon by the Eastern librarians? I have not replied by telegraph but have written to the effect that I have heard nothing of the matter,[2] & would like to know something about it & who is at the bottom of it before giving the use of my name.

It would seem as there was time enough between now and August to arrange such a gathering by correspondence and without coming upon people by telegraph.

Yours very truly
W. F. Poole.

ALS. Superintendent's File, BPL. William Frederick Poole (1821-1894), Librarian, Chicago Public Library, 1874-1887, and subsequently second president of the Association.

[1]*Not located*
[2]*Not located.*

May 19, 1876   [New York]

Got up at 4/45, went to the 5:30 train. Not having passengers enough they did not send it out but made our tickets good on the faster train at 6:30 which I took, getting in Phila. on the grounds at 9:15. I went at once into [1 word missing] and looked for Lindsley[1] but failed to get any clue whatever to him. Then I tried for John Eaton[2] and after ½ hour found him and made an appointment for an hour later. After going about on the narrow gauge railroad I had a long talk with Mr. Eaton. He favors our library project very much, will issue the call for the convention and send it abroad, present the prospectus in the library volume[3] of which they are going to print 10,000 copies and in all proper ways help forward the work. I was greatly pleased at the interest he manifested. After getting through with him I spent the rest of the day till 6:30 in sightseeing, going through the main building . . . . Went to New Brunswick and stayed all night so I might see Prof. Lockwood[4] about metric circular for schools . . . .

———————◦—◦◦●◦—◦———————

Excerpt from entry in Dewey, "Diary," no. 5, Dewey Papers, CUL. Dewey's itinerary during these days (according to his diary): May 16, left Boston early evening, arrived in New York; May 19, early morning, left New York for Philadelphia, spent day in latter city, then spent evening in New Brunswick, New Jersey. May 20, went back to New York. Left New York by boat for Boston, and arrived in the latter city same day.

[1] *Probably David Philip Lindsley (1834-1897), whose system of shorthand, takigraphy, Dewey taught at Amherst.*

[2] *John Eaton (1829-1906), U. S. Commissioner of Education, 1870-1886. He built up the Bureau of Education and especially its statistical and data collecting activities.* Public Libraries in the U. S., *1876, is a monument to his interest in libraries. In addition to the conference, Dewey undoubtedly talked about the* Library Journal *and his decimal classification. He had been in touch with Eaton regarding the latter in late April when Cutter wrote Eaton that he thought Dewey's scheme should be written up for the government report. See Dewey, "Diary," entries for April 11, 27, 28, May 2, 4, 5, 1876.*

[3] *Public Libraries in the U. S., 1876.*

[4] Not identified.

✦ ——————◄◆►—————— ✦

11. WINSOR TO LEYPOLDT

May 19. 76

Dear Sir,–

We are in receipt of your despatch of this date,[1] and beg to say in reply that while we comprehend the advantages from the proposed conference of librarians, we feel unwilling to name any place outside of Boston, to which under the present pressure of official duties, we can be at all sure of going during the present season; altho as Boston may not be considered sufficiently Central for the purpose, we feel we must leave the determination of place and date to you, and then trust to our engagements admitting of the pleasure we might take for participating in the deliberations of the Conference.

AL. Superintendent's File, BPL. Believed to be a carbon in Winsor's handwriting of a letter written to Leypoldt, possibly in answer to a Leypoldt letter of May 19. See item 5 where Dewey indicates an answer to Winsor and Whitney's letter of May 18.

[1]*Not located.*

12. MELVIL DEWEY'S DIARY

May 20, 1876

[New York]

. . . Thence[1] I went off to Leypoldt's again and after a little talk with him went down to K. & S.[2] . . . I then went back to Leypoldt. Poole & the Boston people[3] were all agreed to sign without knowing more of the character of the project and most of those sent to [several words not transcribed] Evans[4] & Fiske[5] telegraphed their names & Noyes[6] of Brooklyn sent in his by Jones.[7] I told him I would look up these fellows here [Boston] & telegraph him Monday [May 22] of the result. Fletcher misunderstood the slip sent him & so we got into an awkward little hole. I telegraphed him as I took the boat for Boston . . . .

Excerpt from entry in Dewey, "Diary," no. 5, Dewey Papers, CUL.

¹*From Van Nostrand's where he had discussed publication of Dr. Frederick A. P. Barnard's book.*

²*Reference uncertain. Apparently these were individuals interested in metric matters. Could the "K." have been Duran Kimball (1842-1907) who wrote books on shorthand based on Lindsley's takigraphy?*

³*This statement is inexplicable. Poole was decidedly not in favor of the project at this point as Dewey later noted, and the letters sent from Boston by Justin Winsor can scarcely be considered endorsements. See items 6 and 11. Not until Dewey visited the Boston Public Library on May 22 did the Bostonians agree to lend their names.*

⁴*See item 8.*

⁵*John Fiske (1842-1901), Assistant Librarian, Harvard University, 1872-1879. Telegram not located.*

⁶*Stephen Buttrick Noyes (1833-1885), Librarian, Mercantile Library Association, Brooklyn, 1858-1885, except for three years at the Library of Congress.*

⁷*Lynds Eugene Jones.*

13. MELVIL DEWEY'S DIARY

May 22, 1876   [Boston]

Came in[1] & went at once to business. Saw Cutter and got his name for call. Went to Public Library & got Winsor, Perkins & Whitney both for call and editors. Then went to Harvard & got Fiske & Sibley[2] & Abbot[3] for call & A. for editor. Fiske promised before. Got pretty tired & went out early to Malden for a little rest.

Excerpt from entry in Dewey, "Diary," no. 5, Dewey Papers, CUL.

[1]*From Malden, where he had rented a room.*

[2]*John Langdon Sibley (1804-1885), Assistant Librarian, 1841-1856, and Librarian, 1856-1877, Harvard University.*

[3]*Ezra Abbot (1819-1884), Assistant Librarian, Harvard, 1856-1871; Professor of New Testament Criticism, Harvard Divinity School, 1872-1884.*

14. PUBLISHERS' WEEKLY *EDITORIAL—* *LIBRARY CO-OPERATION*

It is remarkable, in these days of discussion and co-operation, that, in the library field, where discussion and co-operation could be made so advantageous, there has been so little of either. The librarians of the principal libraries such as Mr. Spofford, Mr. Winsor, Mr. Cutter, Mr. Poole, and others, of course take pains to acquaint themselves with the latest methods of library work, and the inventions or suggestions which may benefit their libraries. But even in their cases, all this is incidental and occasional, and the great body of librarians, who have less opportunity of acquainting themselves with what is going on among others, are those who especially need such help, and who have no means of getting it. In a great library, such as the Boston Public, it is the continual effort of the superintendent to test and utilize every little suggestion of improvement that comes to him or that he can lay hands on; for in the conduct of so large an institution the minutest economy or convenience multiples to so astounding an extent, that a penny or a minute saved in this particular becomes dollars or days gained in the total. Although the smaller libraries can not thus experiment each for itself, it is of the utmost importance that they should get the benefit of the improvements made by the larger ones, which tell proportionately in even greater degree in a small library than in a large one.

The varied and altogether praiseworthy publications of the Boston Public Library[1] have done very much to diffuse among the smaller libraries this sort of information, and we have also made some endeavor in the PUBLISHERS' WEEKLY to represent the general interests of the libraries and the latest improvements in library economy. With more support from the smaller libraries, we should have been able and glad to do this to much greater extent; and it is certainly important that so large and intelligent an interest should have some means of journalistic communication. The PUBLISHERS' WEEKLY serves a useful purpose to librarians, in giving them their commercial and much of their bibliographical information, and in treating of this matter of library management and economy, we have been anxious to develop to the full its possible usefulness in this latter field.

But, within a brief time, the way has been opened for a special American library journal, which it is now proposed to issue, with this office as its publishing base, under the editorial management of a specialist, endorsed for the purpose by leading librarians, and under the auspices of a consulting editorial board of the latter. Of this proposed journal we shall give further particulars as the plans develop, and shall take occasion later to ask from libraries that direct support without which it can not be undertaken. The purpose is to present a library help, which shall save a hundred dollars a year to libraries of any size by the conveniences which it will offer, and it is hoped that the leading libraries will see this with sufficient directness to assure the undertaking of a monthly periodical.

But there is another means of reaching this end, which is not less important, and which was broached in Europe some weeks ago by a correspondent of the London *Academy*. He suggested an International Congress of Librarians, and we would refer our library readers to the interesting points brought forward in his article, which they will find in our issue No. 223, for April 22d. We may say briefly that he urged a meeting of librarians from different countries face to face, where they could exchange ideas in regard to the important matters of the machinery for placing and shifting books, binding, classifying, and cataloguing, etc., etc., in which several specialties the different librarians are of course variously versed. Among his detailed suggestions was the possibility of an international arrangement as to cataloguing, by which English books should be catalogued at the British Museum, French books at the Bibliothèque Nationale, etc., etc., whence, at a trifling expense, printed slips might be sent to each library, of whatever nation, that desire them or took part in the arrangement.

We submit that such a congress of the leading librarians, and as many of the less experienced ones as have a thirst for bibliographical knowledge, and could come, would at least be of decided usefulness; and as it is the fashion to organize Centennial congresses, it is certainly proper to take advantage of the fashion and have a conference at Philadelphia this year. We are glad to state that a preliminary call is being signed by several gentlemen connected with the library interest, for such a congress, and we have no doubt that good will come of it. It is proposed to combine all promising suggestions that come in in reply to this preliminary call in a further address to the library interest, definitely naming the date, and setting forth the points which may usefully be brought up. Such a conference was held in 1853, but since then our libraries have grown tenfold, and there is twenty times the need for co-operation. We are sure that the conference will prove an effective meeting.

Editorial in *Publishers' Weekly*, 9 (May 20, 1876), 632-633. Exact date of mailing of this issue is not known. Edward J. Nolan of Philadelphia said that the issue reached him on June 12 (Nolan to Dewey, ALS, June 12, 1876, not reproduced here), and John Shaw Billings on June 19 (item 37) stated that he received the "call" with his May 20 issue of *PW*, thus implying a mailing date of mid-June, very late for a weekly. However, Dewey in his "Diary," May 18, 1876, states that the library number of *PW* was just ready to print. It seems unlikely that Leypoldt and Bowker would delay the mailing of this issue for almost a month. Rose Weinberg, Librarian, R. R. Bowker Co., believes this editorial was definitely written by Richard Rodgers Bowker, and I concur. Bowker's editorial and financial interests in the *PW* and *LJ* continued until his death in 1933.

[1]*Almost a year earlier the* Publishers' Weekly, *8 (August 14, 1875), 336, had noted that "the Boston Public Library is fast becoming the fountain-head of American bibliographical information, for which it should win the gratitude of the whole reading community."*

15. W. T. PEOPLES TO DEWEY

MERCANTILE LIBRARY
New York, May 24, 1876

Dear Sir:

I approve of the enclosed call and shall endeavor to be present.

Truly yours,
W. T. Peoples
Librarian

ALS. William Thaddeus Peoples (1843-1923), Librarian, New York Mercantile Library, 1873-1916.

---

16. POOLE TO WINSOR

Chicago Public Library, May, 24, 1876

Have from Leypoldt a circular[1] with your name and those of your staff on it. Is this authorized? I inferred you were not for the plan from your note to me.[2] They want my name. I have not given it, for it looks to me as if there were axes to be ground.[3] Leypoldt says you will be asked to draw up a circular. I have written Leypoldt[4] that when you do this, he is authorized to append my name to it.

W.F.P.

Postcard, signed. Superintendent's File, BPL.

[1]*Not located. However, this was probably the preliminary call, item 5, with the names of the Boston Public librarians attached in autograph form. In the first printed call, item 29, the names of Winsor and his staff appear first and Poole's name occurs near the bottom.*

[2]*Not located.*

[3]*Poole was suspicious of book publishers who had adopted a limit of 20% on the discount they would allow libraries, and this probably accounts for his above statement. See W.L. Williamson, William Frederick Poole, 1963, p. 93.*

[4]*Not located.*

41

17. LEYPOLDT TO POOLE

[New York, May 25, 1876]

I certainly owe you an apology. The telegram[1] doubtless needs explanation, coming point blank at you as it did. The reason of our telegraphing instead of writing was that the question had come up just on the eve of the issue of our library number; and it was desired to print the call in that number. We have since concluded, influenced partly by your letter,[2] to speak of the preparation of such a call in the library number, and print the call separately, so as to give more time. We had written for our library number, an editorial on "Library Cooperation" in which such a conference was advocated. As we were nearly ready for the press, Mr. Melvil Dewey, a library enthusiast of the Amherst College Library, came in and said that he had been talking with Mr. Winsor and other leading Boston librarians upon such cooperation, in which they gladly promised to assist. We therefore joined forces in preparing hurriedly a preliminary call[3] a proof of which was forwarded to the leading librarians at the East, while telegrams were sent to yourself, Mr. Vickers, & Mr. Evans.

Direct quote from a letter of Poole to Dewey, ALS, Dec. 28, 1883, Dewey Papers, CUL. Poole quoted from a letter he said was in his possession and threatened to use it against the contention that Dewey originated the conference idea. See introduction.

[1]*Not located.*

[2]*Not located, but also referred to in Poole to Winsor, postcard, May 24, 1876, item 16.*

[3]*Not located.*

18. A. R. SPOFFORD TO LEYPOLDT

LIBRARY OF CONGRESS
Washington, May 29th, 1876

Private

Dear Sir:

I have your Circular[1] regarding a Conference of Librarians at Philadelphia. While I do not think it best to sign such a call officially, because I have always entertained insuperable objections to figuring in conventions (usually mere wordy outlets for impracticables and pretenders) I will cheerfully do my part to co-operate with any well-organized endeavor to aid the whole profession by solid publications, such as your recent articles seem to contemplate.[2] I may also find it possible to look in upon the Conference in August.

I confess that I look with perhaps undue distrust upon mixing the methods of the bibliographer, which are those of patient and accurate research, with the methods of the stump, which are conspicuously the reverse.

> Very respectfully,
> A. R. Spofford
> Librarian of Congress

ALS. Ainsworth Rand Spofford (1825-1908), Librarian of Congress, 1864-1897. Dewey's shorthand notes on verso: "Spofford, A. R. declining to sign call. Answer 76/6/1." Spofford had expressed similar reservations to Commissioner of Education John Eaton with respect to the conference proposal of Thomas Hale Williams, Eaton to Williams, AL, Feb. 6, 1876, Lbk, National Archives. He also did not hesitate to repeat the same views to Poole. See Poole to Winsor, postcard, May 31, 1876, item 22.

[1]*Preliminary call, item 5. Spofford's copy not located.*

[2]*Apparently reference to Leypoldt's library and bibliographical notes sections in* PW, *which began to appear in January, 1876.*

Library of Congress,

Washington, May 29th, 1876

Dear Sir;

I have your Circular regarding a Conference of Librarians at Philadelphia. While I do not think it best to sign such a call officially, because I have always entertained insuperable objections to figuring in conventions (usually mere wordy outlets for impracticables and pretenders) I will cheerfully do my part to co-operate with any well-organised endeavor to aid the whole profession by solid publications, such as your recent articles seem to contemplate. I may also find it possible to look in upon the Conference in August.

I confess that I look with perhaps undue distrust upon mixing the methods of the bibliographer, which are those of patient and accurate research, with the methods of the stump, which are conspicuously the reverse.

Very respectfully,

A. R. Spofford
Librarian of Congress.

F. Leypoldt, Esq.

19. LLOYD P. SMITH TO LEYPOLDT

Library C°. of Philadª., May 29, 1876

Dear Sir,

I did not sign the call for a Librarian's Convention because in the regular course this Library will be closed on 15 Aug. for the regular vacation. I have, however, consulted with some of our Directors who have agreed to change the time somewhat &, if their action is approved by the Board, I can attend & have the Library open for inspection of the Convention. In any event you may sign my name to the call. I was present at the last Convention of Librarians in 1851[1] and got the valuable idea of a card catalogue.

I have given instructions to forward you a copy of vol. 3 of our Catalogue[2] vol. 1 & 2 being out of print. Vol. 3 contains a complete Index to the Library down to the date of publication.

Yours truly,
Lloyd P. Smith
Librarian

Mr. Poole is the proper man to preside.[3] Philadelphia is insufferably hot on the 15 August. Why not have it later?

ALS. Lloyd P. Smith (1882-1886), Librarian, Library Company of Philadelphia, 1851-1886. Dewey's shorthand note: "Smith, L. P. Answer signing call 5/30."

[1] *Date should be 1853.*

[2] *Philadelphia. Library Company.* A Catalogue of Books Belonging to the Library Company of Philadelphia; to which is Prefixed a Short Account of the Institution . . . *Philadephia: C. Sherman, 1835. Vol. III:* Containing the Titles Added from 1835 to 1856. Together with an Alphabetical Index to the Whole. *Philadelphia: Printed for Company, 1856.*

[3] *Poole and Smith had both been members of the 1853 Conference and became very close friends thereafter.*

20. JAMES G. BARNWELL TO LEYPOLDT

327 N. Ninth St.
Philadelphia, May 30th., 1876

Dear Sir:–

I herewith return, signed, the proof "Call for a Library Conference"[1] and most heartily do I endorse the proposition, believing that it will be productive of good.

I have not thought much as to special topics except those that will naturally suggest themselves to every one connected with the management of *large* libraries at least.

The subjects of *cataloguing* and of *printing* the catalogue are of great practical importance. The best method of arranging maps, charts, engravings, &c has always been a perplexing question to the librarian. The utilization of pamphlets is another. But the list is almost endless.

I could here suggest that the wording of the call might be as modified as to embrace "librarians and others interested in bibliography" to borrow the wording of a similar call issued for the convention held in 1853.[2] There are many gentlemen whose presence might be desirable but who would feel some delicacy in considering themselves embraced in the terms of the call without a more explicit phraseology as to the class of persons invited.

Yours respectfully
James G. Barnwell

LS. James G. Barnwell (1833-1919), Director, 1863-1887, and Vice President, 1876-1879, Philadelphia Mercantile Library.

[1] *Barnwell's copy not located.*
[2] *The 1853 Call is reproduced in George B. Utley*, The Librarians' Conference of 1853, *pp. 131-132.*

21. HENRY A. HOMES TO LEYPOLDT

NEW YORK STATE LIBRARY
Albany, May 30, 1876

Dear Sir,

I very cheerfully put my name down as approving of the Librarians' Convention, although I cannot attach as much importance to the coöperation of librarians of state Libraries, as to those of free public libraries. If the Convention is indeed held, I shall certainly aim to be present. Librarians cannot help feeling a professional sympathy with each other and Philadelphia has not only its centennial fixtures, but that of being the home of the most world-renowned citizen of the country, of Franklin, *the Librarian.*

Respectfully yours,
H. A. Homes

ALS. Henry Augustus Homes (1812-1887), Librarian, New York State Library, 1862-1887, and subsequently one of the first vice presidents of the American Library Association.

22. POOLE TO WINSOR

Chicago Public Library, May 31, 1876

Spofford writes that he declined to give his name to the Call, having a distrust of wordy conventions which the stump orator usually captures.[1] I shall follow his example unless you start the thing anew and promise to attend. I am surprised that you gave them your name with the understanding that you did not intend to be present, merely expressing your good wishes. Your name will not be so interpreted. Spofford says Prof. Seely[2] calls Mr. Melvil Dewey "a tremendous talker, and a little of an old maid." It won't pay for you and me to attend that barbecue.

W.F.P.

Postcard, signed. Superintendent's File, BPL.

[1]*See item 18. Spofford's letter to Poole not located, but quoted in Poole to Dewey, ALS, Dec. 28, 1883, Dewey Papers, CUL.*

[2]*Julius H. Seelye (1824-1895), Professor of Philosophy, 1858-1875, and President, 1876-1890, Amherst College.*

23. W. S. BUTLER TO DEWEY

SOCIETY LIBRARY
New York, May 31, 1876

Dear Sir:

I gladly append my name to the call for a Library Conference.

If not able to be present, I would like the liberty of suggesting as a topic for consideration "the best methods of preparing Catalogues for general use."

Very respectfully
W. S. Butler

ALS. Wentworth Sanborn Butler (1826-1910), Assistant Librarian, 1855-1857, and then Librarian, 1855-1895, New York Society Library.

49

24. FREDERICK SAUNDERS TO LEYPOLDT

ASTOR LIBRARY
May 31/76

My Dear Sir,

I certainly owe you an apology for thus delaying to respond to your Circular-"Call": but I have been so pre-occupied that I could not do it until now. I have Mr. Brevoort's[1] ready consent to sign for him.

Very truly yours,
F. Saunders

Thanks for your Catalogues.[2]

ALS. Frederick Saunders (1807-1902), Assistant Librarian, 1859-1876, and then Librarian, 1876-1896, Astor Library, New York.

[1]*James Carson Brevoort (1818-1887), for twenty-six years an active member of the Board of Trustees, Astor Library.*
[2]*Reference uncertain.*

25. CONGRESS OF LIBRARIANS

A special American Library Journal is shortly to be issued from the office of the Publishers' Weekly; and we learn from the same source that steps are being taken to bring about a congress of librarians at Philadelphia during the present year. Their last conference was held in 1853—a date whose remoteness is not expressed by a quarter of a century.

Article, "Notes," *The Nation*, 22 (June 1, 1876), 350, probably written by Charles Ammi Cutter.

26. REUBEN A. GUILD TO LEYPOLDT

LIBRARY OF BROWN UNIVERSITY
Providence, R.I., June 1, 1876

Dear Sir

I return your circular with signatures.[1] It may not be possible for me to attend the Convention, owing to recent and severe trial and bereavement. Still I cordially approve of such a meeting and will gladly aid and encourage to the extent of my ability. During the 28 years that I have been Librarian of this Univ. I have learned some things pertaining to the "Craft." Chief of which is that I have many things yet to learn.

Yours fraternally & truly
Reuben A. Guild

ALS. Reuben Aldridge Guild (1822-1899), Librarian of Brown University, 1848-1893. Guild was a prominent member of the 1853 Conference.

[1]*Guild's copy not located.*

27. DEWEY TO POOLE

[Boston, June 5, 1876]

Mr. Leypoldt wrote to me that you were a little shy of the hurried invitation he sent you about a library conference. I did not wonder; for I was not a little surprised at the prominent place given to my poor name. On the strength of your shyness of the new enterprise I said to Mr. Cutter[1] that I wished he would drop you a note to the effect that he knew me. I am so prominent in the movement simply because no one else could be found willing to do the necessary work without any adequate compensation. We can't do without you and feel satisfied. Your name is always mentioned among the very first, and it would look all wrong not to see it in the list we now have.

Direct quote from a letter of Poole to Dewey, ALS, Dec. 28, 1883, Dewey Papers, CUL. In the same letter, Poole quotes from a letter of Cutter dated June 2 [actually June 5] commending Dewey: "At the request of Mr. Melvil Dewey I write to say that he is no imposter, humbug, speculater, dead beat, or anything of the sort [Did anybody say you were?] I've talked a good deal with Mr. Dewey, and, for a new acquaintance, know him pretty well." Poole cited these letters as proof that he was not opposed to the conference idea, but merely wanted to know who was behind it. He adds that he thinks Leypoldt comes in for a strong claim as originator of the conference idea.

[1]*Dewey, "Diary," June 5, 1876, Dewey Papers, CUL, "Saw Cutter & got a letter from him to Poole commending me & my journal . . . . "*

28. SAMUEL F. HAVEN TO DEWEY

AMERICAN ANTIQUARIAN SOCIETY
Worcester, Mass., June 5, 1876

Dear Sir,

Returning to my office, after a month's absence at the South, I have found on my table the Proof of "A Call for a Library Conference"[1] at Philadelphia on the 15th of August next.

I am certainly very glad of the opportunity to add my name to such a call, as I have a high opinion of the utility of such a meeting.

Yours, Dear Sir,
Very truly
S. F. Haven

ALS. Samuel Foster Haven (1806-1881), Librarian, American Antiquarian Society, 1837-1881. Haven had been an active member of the 1853 Conference.

[1]*Haven's copy not located.*

29. CALL FOR A LIBRARY CONFERENCE (FIRST PRINTED CALL)

CALL FOR A LIBRARY CONFERENCE.

THE undersigned, connected with the library interest of this country, believing that efficiency and economy in library work would be promoted by a conference of librarians, which should afford opportunity for mutual consultation and practical co-operation, issue this preliminary call, inviting librarians and all interested in library and bibliographical work, to meet at Philadelphia, on the 15th of August next, or otherwise as may be found more generally acceptable.

Lack of time forbidding more general consultation by direct correspondence, the present method is used as the most available for soliciting further signatures and suggestions for the preparation of the formal and general call to be issued at a later date. Those approving of the plan and willing to indorse such a call, whether they may be able to be present or not, are requested to send their names, with suggestions as to topics to be presented, etc., to MELVIL DEWEY, care of the PUBLISHERS' WEEKLY, 37 Park Row, New-York.

The place and date suggested are named in view of the usual library vacation about that time, when a large number of librarians would be likely to visit the Centennial Exhibition, with its book and library displays. Those preferring another date or place are requested to signify their choice.

JUSTIN WINSOR, *Boston Public Library.*

J. L. WHITNEY, *Boston Public Library.*

FRED. B. PERKINS, *Boston Public Library.*

C. A. CUTTER, *Boston Athenæum.*

JOHN LANGDON SIBLEY, *Harvard Univ. Libr.*

JOHN FISKE, *Harvard University Library.*

EZRA ABBOT, *Harvard University.*

S. F. HAVEN, *Am. Antiquarian Soc., Worcester.*

J. CARSON BREVOORT, *Astor Library.*

F. SAUNDERS, *Astor Library.*

W. S. BUTLER, *New-York Society Library.*

W. T. PEOPLES, *New-York Mercantile Library.*

JACOB SCHWARTZ, *Apprentices' Library, N.Y.*

S. B. NOYES, *Brooklyn Mercantile Library.*

H. A. HOMES, *New-York State Library.*

LLOYD P. SMITH, *Philadelphia Library Co.*

REUBEN A. GUILD, *Brown University Library.*

J. D. HEDGE, *Providence Athenæum.*

ADDISON VAN NAME, *Yale College Library.*

FRANKLIN B. DEXTER, *Yale College Library.*

A. S. PACKARD, *Bowdoin College Library.*

MELVIL DEWEY, *Amherst College Library.*

JAS. G. BARNWELL, *Philadelphia Merc. Library.*

JOHN EATON, *Bureau of Education, Washington.*

WM. F. POOLE, *Chicago Public Library.*

CHAS. EVANS, *Indianapolis Public Library.*

THOS. VICKERS, *Cincinnati Public Library.*

JNO. N. DYER, *St. Louis Mercantile Library.*

Document. This is the only copy of a conference call in the 1876 scrapbook itself. Another copy of the same printed call has been located in the Bowker Papers of the New York Public Library, although neither copy is dated. However, this call was almost certainly mailed between June 5 and June 10, 1876, with the probable date being either June 8 or 9. John Shaw Billings indicated that the circular was mailed with the *Publishers' Weekly* of May 20, 1876, although this seems unlikely (item 37). Bowker was in Boston on June 8-10, 1876, and discussed library matters including a circular (probably the LJ prospectus) but there is no mention of the mailing of this document. Dewey, "Diary," June 8-10, 1876, Dewey Papers, CUL. Samuel F. Haven, Librarian of the American Antiquarian Society, gave permission for the use of his name on the circular in a letter of June 5 (item 28). It is hardly likely that Leypoldt would have gone to press with the circular until Haven's favorable reply had been received, especially in view of the earlier difficulty with the unauthorized use of Fletcher's name. In the scrapbook are one postcard and three letters dated June 10, 1876, and referring to the circular. All four are from cities in the East where the circular could have been mailed from New York and received at any of the four libraries within two days. Hannah P. James' letter to Dewey (item 30) refers specifically to his suggestion that librarians could combine the convention trip with their vacations, an idea not contained in the preliminary "proof" call (item 5). The circular elicited numerous letters and cards in mid-June, 1876.

The reasons for the presence of most of the names appearing on the circular are easily determined: the major librarians and the major geographic areas are represented. The only major omission is the name of A. R. Spofford, Librarian of Congress.

Of the 28 names on the circular, twelve did not attend the conference, including the Harvard librarians, General Eaton, and Haven. Nineteen subsequently joined the American Library Association, according to the 1879 membership list, including Perkins, Packard, Haven, Hedge, and Dyer who did not go to Philadelphia.

Except for a slight change in the order of the names, this same list appeared on the revised circular issued in late July, 1876 (item 62). Interestingly enough, three of the four names which appeared on the preliminary "proof" call (item 5) do not appear on this or the revised circular: Leypoldt, Fletcher, and Jones. All had joined the Association by 1879, though Jones was the only one of the three present at Philadelphia.

Librarians not otherwise identified in the footnotes: Alpheus Spring Packard (1798-1884), Professor and Librarian, Bowdoin College, 1869-1881; John N. Dyer (1833-1889), Librarian, Mercantile Library of St. Louis, 1862-1889.

30. HANNAH P. JAMES TO DEWEY

NEWTON FREE LIBRARY
June 10th '76

Dear Sir-

The circular issued by the "Publisher's Weekly" containing a "Call for a Library Conference"[1] has been received, and in answer to the request for communications from Librarians I will say, that I approve most heartily of the Call—and shall hope to be present at the meeting if one is held—

I cannot hope to add anything to the value and interest of the occasion—but—I am sure much can be learned from the veterans of the Corps—which will be valuable—One thing I would like to say—that I think a later date would be more agreeable than the 15th of Aug—Phila. must be a very hot place at that time—and I am afraid that a *"vacation"* spent in sight-seeing during such warm weather would hardly prepare a Librarian for another year's Campaign—Speaking for myself—I wish to *rest* at the mountains in Aug—& would like when the weather is cooler—say in Sept—or the first of Oct—to go to Phila. I give my preference as you ask particularly each one's opinion—

Whatever time tho is decided upon, I shall hope to be there.

Yours truly
Hannah P. James
Librarian Newton Free Library

———————•◄◄►►◄———————

ALS. Hannah Packard James (1835-1903), Librarian, Newton, Mass., Free Library, 1870-1887. Miss James did not attend, but the Sup't., Frederick Jackson, did attend as official delegate of the trustees.

[1]*Item 29. See Frederick Jackson to Dewey, ALS, Sept. 9, 1876, in the scrapbook but not reproduced here.*

31. JAMES W. WARD TO DEWEY

GROSVENOR LIBRARY
Buffalo, N.Y., June 12, 1876

Dr Sir

I cheerfully add my name, on behalf of this Library, to your call for a Librarian's Convention; especially as it is a matter towards a public suggestion of which, I had myself, in consultation already taken some preliminary steps. I have now only to fall into line in cordial co-operation with the call you have issued.

As you request suggestions as to time and place, in regard to the time proposed, I would say, that it has this objection, that it coincides with the time appointed for the meeting of the American Association for Adv. of Science, in this city—which is to take place on the 16th of August, and continue one week. American Microscopists have been also invited to meet here the same week for the purpose of a general systematic organization: in this last project, I have, for one, a personal and functional interest; and the two calls, I should judge, must include others of our fraternity.

At all events, would it not be better, not to encroach on the field day of the Am. Association? In which case, how would a week earlier (or later,) than you have proposed, do?

> I am very cordially
> Jas. W. Ward
> Librn.

ALS. James W. Ward (1816-1897), Librarian, Grosvenor Public Library, Buffalo, 1874-1896. Dewey's shorthand note: "Ward, James W. 76/6/19."

32. S. S. GREEN TO DEWEY

Worcester, Mass. June 13, 1876

Dear Sir,

In response to the circular relating to a "Library Conference" I send you my name to be added to the list of those who approve the plan.

My observation of conventions held by educational and religious bodies has led me to believe that, often, such assemblies while useful for social purposes do not advance greatly the interests which it was the aim to promote in convening them. The time of these conventions is too much taken up in listening to remarks by second and third rate men.

It is very gratifying, therefore, to find that in a case where success depends so largely upon a proper initiation of the arrangements as it does in the present undertaking persons are making these who will lay out *work* for the convention and bring into prominence in its deliberations the blest [sic] of the members of what we hope will soon be the fraternity of librarians.

Much good may certainly be done by bringing librarians together and organizing them and this movement should be heartily seconded and the proposed plan faithfully tried.

Speaking for myself alone I should prefer to attend a convention a little later in the season, say in September or October, but shall try to be present at whatever time it is concluded to hold one.

Respectfully yours
Samuel S. Green
Librarian

ALS. Samuel Swett Green (1837-1918), Librarian, Free Public Library, Worcester, Mass., 1871-1909. Green was subsequently one of the most diligent supporters of the Association, attending all the national conventions from 1876 to 1894 and serving as president in 1891.

33. R. B. POOL TO DEWEY

YOUNG MEN'S CHRISTIAN ASSOCIATION
New York, June 13th 1876

Dear Sir.

In response to the circular calling for a Conference of Librarians, I beg to express my hearty approval of the project-

I believe great service may be done the library interests of the country by such a gathering—Phila. is certainly a most appropriate place—I should prefer the first of Aug. as the time for the convention as I should in all probability be East, on my vacation, at the time mentioned—15 Aug.

If I may suggest any topics, I would mention the following:

The desirability of a *Classified Catalogue*, on the alphabetical system (e.g.—the Harvard College Catalogue, card)[1]

Card Catalogues—their advantages, and the best mechanical appliances for their use (note M. Bonnange's of Paris—elucidated in a brochure entitled—Projet d'un Catalogue Universal de,)[2]

Statistics—The use they subserve & the extent to which they should be kept

Exchanges—How can they more be generally promoted?

There are a good many minor questions which might be dealt with, I think, in an informal way—by asking questions verbally—and such persons responding as could throw any light on the subject.

Many librarians would be grateful for light on little perplexing questions of detail—such as the order of the library—treatment of bummers, protection of books, etc.

I am
Yours truly
R. B. Pool
Librn.

ALS. Reuben Brooks Pool (1834-1895), Librarian, Y.M.C.A., New York, 1864-1895.

[1]*For a discussion of Ezra Abbot's alphabetico-classed catalogue see Jim Ranz*, The Printed Book Catalogue in American Libraries: 1723-1900 (ACRL *Monograph No. 26; Chicago: American Library Association, 1964), pp. 60-61, 70-72.*

[2]*Ferdinand Bonnange*, Le bilan de l'esprit humain. Projet d'un catalogue universel des productions intellectuelles. Mémoire sur les moyen à employer pour dresser rapidement des catalogues exacts et complets des richesses renfermées dans les bibliothèques, les dépôts d'archives et les musées et collections. *Paris: Gauthier-Villars, 1874. 39p. See the discussion of M. Bonnange's system at the conference, ALJ, 1 (Nov. 30, 1876), 131.*

34. POOLE TO DEWEY

PUBLIC LIBRARY OF CHICAGO
Chicago, June 15, 1876

Dear Sir.

Your letter of the 12th inst. is recd.[1] As you desire some suggestions from me as to the conference, I will make them.

I am too far away to be on the executive committee. Mr. Winsor must be on it, & must be the leading spirit. When it is understood that the purpose of the conference is mainly for getting acquainted with each other, and not for general [1 word ill.][2] and showing up patent rights, Mr. Spofford, I think, could be induced to be a member of the committee. If it is to be held in Phil., Mr. Smith should be the chairman of, at least, the subcommittee to do the local work, and with Mr. John Edmands,[3] or Mr. Barnwell of the Mercantile Library, to help him. A few papers with discussions upon the subject afterwards, would perhaps be all the business it would be well to go into. Have the names of the general committee those that do not need to be introduced to the public or the library profession. Don't undertake to carry out the plan unless there is to be united action. It won't do for the Boston Public Library *to give their names* and then *stay away*.

The date of the meeting had best be put off till the weather is comfortable in Phil. I should say September. The new Ridgway Library building in Phil. would then be nearly finished. I have no doubt that the Phil. people would be very hospitable and would make it very pleasant to their visitors. For that reason I should wish that there be a strong local committee to manage that part of the business.

I throw out these ideas simply as suggestions. You will please leave me off the Committee of Arrangements. Not that I should be unwilling to do the work, but because it is desirable that the main agreement should be in the hands of a few persons who can meet and consult, and thus act with promptness & efficiency. Make Winsor the head & a mistake will not be likely to occur.

Yours truly

W. F. Poole

ALS.

[1]*Not located.*

[2]*Word illegible, but begins "blo---." Presumably Poole intends some variation of "blowing" or boasting.*

[3]*John Edmands (1820-1915), Librarian, Mercantile Library of Philadelphia, 1856-1901. Barnwell was Vice President of the Mercantile Library. Both participated actively in the conference.*

35. WILLIAM E. FOSTER TO DEWEY

TURNER LIBRARY, RANDOLPH, MASS.
June 17, 1876

Dear Sir,-

The circular containing the preliminary call for a library conference, mailed to me, at Hyde Park, has been forwarded to me at this library.

The plan is one that meets my hearty approval; as I believe must be the case with all librarians who have studied at all the practical workings of a library.

I regret exceedingly that the work on the catalogue of this library,[1] which I am now engaged in preparing, will probably be in such a stage of advancement at the time proposed, as to render it impossible for me to leave.

I trust, however, that full reports of the discussions will be printed, to which those who are similarly unfortunate with myself may have access.

I enclose a few of the points which I should be glad to see discussed; and am, with much respect, yours, etc.

W. E. Foster

ALS. William Eaton Foster (1851-1930), Cataloger, Turner Free Library, Randolph, Mass., 1876-1877, and part-time employee of the Boston Public Library concurrently. He was subsequently first librarian of the Providence, R. I., Public Library, 1877-1930. Foster not only attended the conference but read Thomas H. Rogers' paper for him. ALJ, 1 (Nov. 30, 1876), 62-63, 112.

[1] *Turner Library, Randolph, Mass.* Catalogue of the Turner Free Library, Randolph, Mass. (*Boston: A. Mudge & sons, printers, 1877*).

36. FOSTER'S SUGGESTIONS

Topics suggested for discussion

1.—How far should a public library place local restrictions upon the use of its privileges?

2.—What system of charging the loan and return of books combines in the highest degree dispatch, convenience, simplicity, inexpensiveness, and absolute trustworthiness?

3.—To what extent should a printed catalogue be a mere index, and how far may descriptive features be embodied in it?

4.—How can copies of all state and government documents be more effectually secured to public libraries?

5.—In what way is a reform possible in the present showy, but unsubstantial and unsatisfactory style of binding in which publishers send their books into the market?

William E. Foster

ADS.

37. JOHN SHAW BILLINGS TO DEWEY

WAR DEPARTMENT
Surgeon General's Office
Washington, D. C., June 19, 1876

Dear Sir:-

I have received the "Call for a Library Conference" issued with the "Publishers' Weekly" of May 20th, and as suggested write to say that I approve of the plan—and of the place and date of meeting and hope to be present at the meeting which cannot fail to be interesting and instructive. I send you by this mail a specimen of a Catalogue,[1] the preface to which indicates one or two of the points upon which I should like to obtain the opinion of the Conference.

I would request that I may be furnished with any programmes, circulars, &c, relating to the proposed conference as soon as they are issued.

> Very truly yours
> J. S. Billings
> Asst. Surgeon, U.S.A.
> Librarian S.G. Office

ALS. John Shaw Billings (1838-1913), Librarian of the Surgeon General's Office, 1864-1896, and subsequently first director of the New York Public Library.

[1] *This specimen was presented to the conference by Dr. John Ashhurst, Jr., in Billings' absence.* ALJ, *1* (*Nov. 30, 1876*), *121-22.*

38. EMILY F. CARNES TO DEWEY

FREE LIBRARY
Galveston, Texas, June 20th, '76

Dear Sir

I have received the "Call for a Library Conference" & respond with great pleasure, regretting only that distance & other duties will prevent me from having the pleasure of a personal attendance.

But I beg to be permitted to put in one or two suggestions in behalf of the interests of smaller Libraries which with limited means are striving to create the little rills eventually to form the broad stream of public culture.

Cataloguing. To us smaller folk, the plan of a printed book slip in proper size & style for a slip catalogue to be issued with each book, as proposed by the "Publisher's Weekly,"[1] meets my unqualified approbation. It will be an immense advantage to all smaller Librarians who vastly outnumber the larger & more learned ones. It will, moreover, have the beneficial effect of introducing a uniformity of catalogue, which, even if it should not be the entirely best, will be a great benefit.

In this connection I would enquire if it would not be an improvement in the excellent Bulletin of the Boston Public Library to insert the shelf numbers of the cross references. When I merely want to find the numbers to give for "Outis," it is a little annoying to be told to "see Edwards, Joseph."[2] Why not give me the numbers right there?

Classifying. It is to be hoped that the Conference will not confine its attention to a minute system of Classifying which can be adopted only in very large collections. The smaller Libraries, & particularly we smaller Librarians, who are the many, need some sensible system for our use. In the arrangement of the Galveston Library, in the absence of any general plan, we finally adopted the following, which has been found to work reasonably well, each division being open to as many subdivisions as we find necessary.

(See enclosed slip)[3]

In connection with this subject, I would state for the benefit of those Librarians who are compelled to work in limited space & scanty shelfroom, that we have found great advantage in classifying our books for shelf location, & place those of one size together. We have found economy in grading the books from four inches to twelve inches, with a quarter inch grade, making thirty six grades. Books larger than twelve inches, are few. In this way, each book, after being covered, is classified for grade of shelf within its subject division. We thus can place the shelves much nearer together, leaving less room for dust, & placing the most books in a given number of square inches.

I submit these suggestions with great diffidence & only regret that I cannot have the pleasure of attending the conference in person. Hoping it will result in a permanent organization of our useful guild,

I remain Very Respectfully

Emily F. Carnes
Lib'n.

———————— ·◄◖►◄ ————————

ALS. Mrs. Emily F. Carnes, Librarian, Free Library, Galveston, Texas, 1871 until sometime after 1876. Her exact period of service and dates of birth and death not known.

[1]*Item 14.*
[2]*Boston Public Library*, Bulletin, *no. 35 (October, 1875), 415, 405.*
[3]*Missing from scrapbook.*

39. *DEWEY TO WINSOR*

AMERICAN LIBRARY JOURNAL
Boston Office
June 23, 1876

Dear Sir:

I wrote Mr. Poole & Mr. Smith[1] after leaving you yesterday telling them of their choice by our informal votes, to act as the Com. of Arrangements.

I took the liberty of suggesting that as I had handed the letters to you, you would probably write them very soon in order that place and date might be settled definitely & at once.

If you will advise me of the decision of the Committee giving if possible the hour & hall where the meeting will be held I will see that all the libraries are notified at once.

So many are planning for Aug. 15 that we ought to get the later date off at the earliest moment.

Any help that I can afford will be readily rendered.

Hoping for an early decision I am—

Very truly
Melvil Dewey

ALS.

[1] *Letters not located.*

The Secretary Prods the Chairman

Office of the
AMERICAN LIBRARY JOURNAL.

PUBLICATION OFFICE: F. Leypoldt, 37 Park Row (Address, Box 4295), New-York.
BOSTON OFFICE: Melvil Dewey (Managing Editor), 13 Tremont Place
(Address, Box 1667), Boston.

Mr Vinson.   June 23 1876

Dear Sir. I wrote
Mr Poole & Mr Smith after
leaving you yesterday letting
them of their choice by our
informal votes, to act as the
Com. of Arrangements.

I took the liberty of suggesting
that as I had handed the
letters to you, you would
probably write them very soon
in order that place & date
might be settled definitely
& at once.

If you will advise me of
the decision of the Committee
giving if possible the hour &
hall where the meeting will

be held & will see that all
the libraries are notified
at once

So many are planning
for Aug 1st that we ought
to set the later date off at
the earliest moment.

Any help that I can
afford will be readily
rendered.

Hoping for an early
decision I am —

Very truly

Melvil Dewey

40. SMITH TO DEWEY

LIBRARY C⁰ OF PHILAD.ᴬ
Philadelphia, June 24, 1876

My dear Sir,

I accept with pleasure a place on the Committee of Arrangements. I have written to T. Morris Perot,[1] President of the Mercantile Library here, for permission for the convention to use their Lecture Room as a place of meeting.

The Ridgway Branch of the Phila. Library on South Broad St.— costing $900,000 will be so far advanced by the 15th August that the Convention can visit the building and get an idea not only of its size & external appearance, but of its internal arrangements. It is a noble structure.

I beg you will present my cordial regards to my friend Winsor & assure him who, I presume is the Chairman of our Committee, that he can call on me freely for any service in my power.

This Library will be closed from July 19th to Aug. 12th when I shall be away from the city. I expect to go to the Isles of Shoals[2] with my family. I will probably spend one day, say July 20—in Boston, when I shall be glad to confer with you and Mr. Winsor. What house would you advise me to stop at? (Will Mr. Winsor kindly answer this question? Dewey)

Yours cordially
Lloyd P. Smith

ALS. At top of page: "Please preserve this letter for me, with the others. M.D."

[1] *Thomas Morris Perot (1828-1902), President of the Mercantile Library, 1861-1900.*

[2] *Maine and New Hampshire islands, 10 mi. S.E. Portsmouth, N.H.*

41. JOHN JAY BAILEY TO [DEWEY?]

PUBLIC SCHOOL LIBRARY
St. Louis, June 24, 1876

Dear Sir,

Your favor of 16th, recd.[1] I shall look impatiently for the first no. of the Journal, & give it a glad welcome & all the assistance in my power. Please send me some circulars, as soon as out. As for the Convention, I think Aug. 15th the very best time. In October, Librarians are, or ought to be too busy to go to Conventions.

Very respectfully
Jno. Jay Bailey
Librarian

ALS. John Jay Bailey (b. 1833), Librarian, Public School Library of St. Louis, 1865-1877. Bailey apparently took his own advice, for his name does not appear among the registrants for the October Conference. Bailey was replaced as Librarian of the St. Louis Public School Library by Frederick M. Crunden in January, 1877. See ALJ, I (Feb. 28, 1877), 221.

[1]*Not located.*

42. EVANS TO DEWEY

PUBLIC LIBRARY June 24th
Ind'n'pl's, Ind.

Dear Sir:

The 15th of August would certainly be my preference for the date of the Convention, and Justin Winsor of the Boston P.L., Wm. F. Poole of the Chicago P.L. and Lloyd P. Smith of the Philadelphia

Library Company, a good Committee of arrangements. The latter is jolly, companionable, and *at home*. You can fully appreciate the weight that the other two members would give to such a Committee.

Very truly yours,
Charles Evans

Postcard, signed.

43. SMITH TO DEWEY

LIBRARY CO. OF PHILADA.
Philadelphia, June 25, 1876

My dear Sir,

Your favor 16 ins. is at hand.[1]

I am decidedly in favor of Oct. for the Librarians' Conference, although I have made my arrangements to have this Library open on the 15 Aug.—contrary to the usual plan, which is to close three weeks in August. The Mercantile Library in this city has a Lecture Room in its building which might be used for the meetings of the Librarians' Convention. The active man in that Institution is T. Morris Perot, President: the bibliographical director is James G. Barnwell, who, I see, has signed the call. He would be a good chairman of the Committee of Arrangements in this city.

Yours cordially
Lloyd P. Smith

ALS.

[1]*Not located.*

72

PUBLIC LIBRARY OF CHICAGO
Chicago, June 26, 1876

My dear Sir

Yours of the 22d is recd.[1]

The point I have most been interested in, as regards the management of the Conference, is that Mr. Winsor would consent to be at the head of the committee. The next was that Mr. Lloyd P. Smith should be the next man. If Mr. Winsor should think, however, that a resident of Phil. ought to be the chairman, there would [be] reason in it; but I think the other plan is the best. As I have insisted that Mr. Winsor should take command, and [he] has consented, it seems to be right that he should choose his associates. You say that Mr. Winsor desires me to represent the West on the Committee of Arrangements. I will frankly say that under such a leader I will accept, and will do what I can to forward the enterprise.

August 15 I think is out of the question. Sept. may be very warm. Hence I think October is the best appointment to make.

Yours very truly
William F. Poole

ALS.

[1]*Not located, but see Dewey to Winsor, item 39.*

73

PUBLIC LIBRARY
Taunton, Mass., June 26/76

Dear Sir:

In reply to the call for a library conference, I write to say that my engagements at the time of the proposed meeting will preclude my attendance, but as the Committee invite suggestions I venture to propose one subject for discussion which involves the convenience of both librarians and readers—an uniform system of classification. At this time when our National Bureau of Education is understood to be maturing some plan of the kind it is appropriate that those immediately concerned should show their interest in the labor, and, if possible, add to the value and acceptability of its results.

In many of the catalogues, coming under my observation of late, I find no scheme of classification. Individual works are each placed under some one of the smaller heads, but these minor categories are not themselves classified, and arranged under more generic ones, whereby related subjects are grouped in a consistent order. They strike me very much as would an atlas in which the subdivisions of a State were accurately portrayed, but which should fail to indicate the features of the entire country at one view, showing the relative position of the various parts to the whole, and the points of contact with neighboring provinces. The young student is not to be supposed capable of pursuing a given line of investigation into all its collateral branches and if the catalogue is to be really an aid to him, it should exhibit that kind of mapping out.

The importance of bibliographical aid cannot well be overestimated, requiring, as their preparation does, accuracy of information in every department of science, literature and art. Unfortunately, there are few subjects of which there is less adequate popular appreciation than bibliography; and even professed librarians are often at variance on some points for the lack of recognized authorities. Those who have attained proficiency in their profession will doubtless ascribe it more to a natural taste united with a long-continued practical study of its requirements, than to facilities deemed essential by candidates for other professions demanding less varied if more profound accomplishments.

At the same time I would not ignore some valuable contributions towards such a literature. None of us, I presume, will forget the debt of

;ratitude we owe the late Prof. Jewett[1] for instance, for the light he shed
on this difficult and comprehensive theme.

Hoping the coming convention may be one of entire harmony, and
productive of great good to the interests we have at heart, I am yours
respectfully

E. C. Arnold

ALS. Ebenezer Cary Arnold (d. 1901), Librarian, Taunton, Mass.,
Public Library, 1876-1895.

[1]*See Ranz,* The Printed Book Catalogue in American Libraries:
1723-1900, ch. III-IV.

46. DEWEY TO WINSOR

AMHERST COLLEGE LIBRARY
Amherst, Mass., June 27, 1876

Dear Sir,

I enclose a note just at hand from Mr. Smith.[1] Warren[2] writes me
this morning that our *Prospectus* must be there Wed. (to-morrow) so I
fancy the vol. is going to press.

It is very desirable that we get the formal call with date & place of
meeting out at once. The program can be delayed if desirable, for we
shall send our first number of the *Journal* very widely with program in it.

If we had date & place we cd send the *Call* with the volume without
expense & that's a strong argument.

I have quite a quantity of *Calls* like the enclosed which I thot of sending with a corrected date.[3] Do you think it desirable to add more signatures to this call or is better to simply sign the Committees name and
say *generally signed* by prominent librarians.

Our last man is now in line. Spofford writes a cordial letter of acceptance & goes on the Board of Editors.[4]

I sent a pkg. of letters to you as I left town. Did you get them?

Hoping the Com. will fix the date as soon as practicable (& as late in the season I might add for my personal preference)
I am very truly

Melvil Dewey

ALS.

¹*Item 43.*

²*Samuel R. Warren, who, with Major S. N. Clark, edited the U. S. Bureau of Education,* Public Libraries in the U. S., *1876. Dewey's reference is to the prospectus of the* Library Journal *rather than the conference call. The prospectus appeared on pp. xxviii–xxx of the government report.*

³*Apparently a copy of the conference call with the August 15 date crossed out and the October date added. Enclosure missing.*

⁴*Not located.*

47. WINSOR TO DEWEY

BOSTON PUBLIC LIBRARY
Boston, June 28, 1876

Dear Sir, -

I got your package of letters; and the one from L. P. Smith,¹ enclosed by you from Amherst, today. I have been too busy to give time to communicating with Poole & Smith, but will do so today. I think we shall have to use you as Secy of the Committee for detaild work. I will let you know as soon as the day is fixed. Smith will have to arrange for the place in Phil. I am glad to hear of Spofford wheeling into line.

Yours
Justin Winsor.

ALS. Dewey's shorthand notes: "76/6/29 Answer Conference Committee 6/30."

¹*Item 43.*

48. DEWEY TO WINSOR

Amherst, Mass., June 29, 1876

Dear Sir,

I have a few more letters which I enclose. Please preserve for me with the others.

Poole having accepted you are now thoroughly organized for work. Hope to hear the date soon.

Very truly
Melvil Dewey

ALS.

49. POOLE TO WINSOR

PUBLIC LIBRARY OF CHICAGO
Chicago, July 1, 1876

My dear Winsor

Yours of the 28th ult. is rec'd.[1] I have written to Dewey that I would accept to act with you and Mr. L. P. Smith.

As to the date, I entirely agree with you that August is out of the question, and that October is better than September. Let us say October, and leave Mr. Smith to fix the precise date.

I am very glad the matter of the Phil. Conference has now got into such shape that the public and the library interests of the country will have entire confidence in it. The change in Mr. Spofford's views is evidence of this. What do you think of having a few papers prepared and read, with conversations upon them? For instance, there is a vast deal of misconception in the public mind, and especially among our best and most cultivated men, as to the propriety of circulating novels in our public libraries. It is a misconception which yields when the facts are fully presented to them.

In our Chicago Literary Club, (made up of our best literary men numbering 150) we have one evening in the month devoted to conversation on some given topic. Some two months ago Mr. E. C. Larned,[2] one of our most accomplished men and best talkers, proposed to me (Chairman of Com. on Exercises) the subject of "Novels." I gladly consented, and made that the subject of an evenings conversation. Mr. Larned agreed to open. He has positive, very positive views as to their debasing influence, & he has talked and written publicly upon it. We had a very full meeting, and they embraced the best men in the city. Mr. Larned opened in his elegant and forcible style. The President Judge Lawrence[3] called on me to follow, which I did. You know the ground so well, you can imagine what I said. I took the most positive and advanced ground, and as I went on I could see that they were ideas entirely new to the members, and trust that they made an impression upon them. The result was a little singular. Some twenty or more spoke, and not one followed the views of Mr. Larned, but took the other side. Mr. L. had said that Fiction was injurious because *it was not true.* I replied by defending the thesis that there was in literature nothing true but *Fiction.* When the conversation was over many persons came to me and said their opinions had entirely changed.

Now can't you write a paper on that subject? Can't we get Spofford to write a paper?

I enclose Mr. Smith's letters as you desire.

Yours very truly
William F. Poole

―――――――――

ALS. Poole included a section on fiction in his conference paper and a lively discussion ensued. "Some Popular Objections to Public Libraries," ALJ, 1 (Nov. 30, 1876), 45-51, 96-101.

[1]*Not located.*

[2]*Edwin Channing Larned (1820-1884), Chicago lawyer. According to Frederick William Gookin,* The Chicago Literary Club; A History of Its First Fifty Years *(Chicago: Printed for the Club, 1926), p. 267, Larned led a conversation on " The Influence of Modern Fiction," on March 11, 1876.*

[3]*Charles B. Lawrence (1820-1883), Chicago lawyer and at one point Chief Justice of Illinois Supreme Court.*

50. SMITH TO WINSOR

LIBRARY C⁰ OF PHILAD<u>A</u>
Philadelphia, July 1, 1876

My dear Sir,

Your favor is at hand. I am glad you are going to make the time October instead of August. I would suggest Wednesday, Thursday, & Friday the 4-5- & 6- October at which time we can have the use, I doubt not, of the Mercantile Library Lecture room. If not, there will be no difficulty in getting a room to meet in.

I propose to call on you on the morning of the 20 ins.

Yours very truly
Lloyd P. Smith

ALS. Written across top of letter: "Does Mr. Poole agree to this. J. Winsor. Please return this."

51. SOLON F. WHITNEY TO DEWEY

WATERTOWN, MASS., 5th JULY, 1876

Dear Sir,

The library conference proposed for 15th Aug. at Phil. seems to me to be in every way desirable.

I know of no way in which the cause of education and progress can be so easily advanced as in promoting the work of free public libraries. The names of those appended to your circular are a sufficient warrant of able discussions of questions which should draw a large concourse of librarians and library officers from all parts of the country.

The time proposed is the best possible, coming the week before the meeting of the A.A. for Adv. of Science at Buffalo.

I shall certainly attend if no unforseen thing prevents.[1]

Please forward me any notices you may issue previous to the meeting.

I would suggest among the questions to be discussed

(1) The best way of putting libraries on an equality with small traders (who buy for less) in their arrangement for terms in the purchase of books[2]

(2) The advantage to *publishers and those interested* in the spread of copies of good books in the land from having all such in all public libraries where they can be seen as soon as published

(3) The name of Ezra Abbot, Justin Winsor, C. A. Cutter on your circular, if it means their presence and active cooperation, will ensure the discussion of many vexed questions which all libraries would do well to hear discussed such as the best methods of cataloguing, arranging, & issuing books. Mr. Winsor is doing a great work in popularizing public libraries, and will find common ground on which it will be for the interests of *publishers*, *libraries* and *people* to act.

Speed the convention of librarians say I,

Solon F. Whitney, Librarian
Watertown Free Public Library

ALS. Dewey's shorthand on verso: "Omitting the M. F. [?] Suggestions conference. 76/7/13 answered 13." Solon Franklin Whitney (1831-1917), Librarian, Watertown, Mass., Free Public Library, 1868-1917.

[1]*Whitney first had "health" instead of "no unforseen thing," but scratched through that word.*

[2]*Solon Whitney did not attend the conference, but became a member of the Association and attended the convention in New York the following year. Poole's resolution on the 20% discount allowed libraries by booksellers must have been of considerable interest to Whitney. "Proceedings," ALJ, 1 (Nov. 30, 1876), 134-138.*

52. GEORGE L. BURLEY TO SMITH

OFFICE OF THE BOARD OF TRADE
Mercantile Library Building
Philadelphia, July 5th 1876

Dear Sir,

You can have the use of the room of the Board of Trade for a few days beginning on 15th Aug. next at Ten Dolls. per day. If used in the evening there will be two Dolls., Extra charged for each evening, say $12.

Please inform me if you will take the room at these figures. I am not at liberty to take less.

Of course, myself and assistant would not be excluded from the room, in the transaction of the business of the Board.

Yours very truly
Geo. L. Burley
Secy.

ALS. George L. Burley, Secretary, Board of Trade, Mercantile Library Building. One can imagine the reaction of someone like Poole to this suggestion when many librarians were making less than $600 per year!

53. SMITH TO WINSOR

LIBRARY C? OF PHILAD?
Philadelphia, July 6, 1876

My dear Sir,

Your favor 4 ins. is at hand.[1]

I named the 4-5-&6-Oct because my first Assistant is going to be married a little later and will take a holiday.

At this moment only two subjects occur to me for papers to be read. One is the qualification of a good Librarian on which I may write a short paper[2] & the other is the best method of arranging books on the shelves. Perhaps Mr. Spofford of Washington will take that.

I enclose a reply from the person who controls the Lecture Room of the Mercantile Library.[3] I had supposed we could get it free & I still hope to get some place, perhaps the Historical Society, without expense. It will be time enough to attend to that matter two months hence.

Yours very truly
Lloyd P. Smith

I propose to call on you about 11 A.M. on the 20th ins. on my way to Appledore.[4] Since writing the within I have ascertained that we can meet in the charming rooms of the Historical Society without cost.

ALS.

[1]*Not located.*

[2]*Lloyd P. Smith, "The Qualifications of a Librarian," ALJ, 1 (Nov. 30, 1876), 69-74.*

[3]*Item 52.*

[4]*Appledore Island, one of the islands in the Isles of Shoals, S.E. of Portsmouth, N. H. See item 40.*

54. POOLE TO WINSOR

PUBLIC LIBRARY OF CHICAGO
Chicago, July 7, 1876

My dear Winsor.

The date suggested by Mr. Smith (4th, 5th, & 6th of October) for the Conference at Phil. is excellent, and I agree to it. Your letter is rec'd.[1] What you say about introducing anything polemic[2] and that will raise controversy, expresses my views. My idea was that you or somebody big enough to treat the subject in an *unpolemic* way, and that would impart some needed information and matter that is very little understood, was the thing needed. Perhaps the best way will be to let it alone as you suggest. If it comes up we can treat it judiciously and effectively in conversation. While Mr. Bailey of St. Louis is in the main right, I think he was not judicious in presenting the case.[3]

I have just rec'd. the proof of my paper in Mr. Eaton's book on Libraries.[4] It was sent to him more than a year ago. I hope the book will be out soon. The finances of Chicago are in a very bad way, and the stringency is pinching this library fearfully. We are buying no books and have not had our salaries paid for three months. What the outcome will be we can't forsee.

Yours very truly
W. F. Poole.

ALS.

[1] *Not located.*

[2] *Reference to Poole's views on fiction? See item 49.*

[3] *Reference not identified. Bailey's topics in the government report were descriptive, not controversial. Was he already having difficulties with his trustees? See* ALJ, *1 (Feb. 28, 1877), 221.*

[4] *Poole, "The Organization and Management of Libraries," in* Public Libraries in the U.S., *1876, pp. 476-504. Commissioner John Eaton had undertaken the compilation of this work in 1874.*

55. SMITH TO [WINSOR?]

The rooms of the Historical Society are in the Hospital Grounds, Spruce above 8. Their capacity is good—Say 150 persons which will I presume be more than we shall have.

Hoping to see you Monday next.

> Yours
> Lloyd P. Smith
> 7/14/76

Postcard, signed.

56. S. N. CLARK TO DEWEY

DEPARTMENT OF THE INTERIOR
Bureau of Education
Washington, D. C., July 14, 1876

Dear Sir:

General Eaton[1] has returned and says that you may send printed copies of the call for the Library Convention here and we will send them out to the libraries. It will be well for you to get them here by the 1st of August if you can. Regarding the sending out of the prospectus from here there is some hesitation.[2] If General Eaton decides favorably I will let you know.

> Yours truly
> S. N. Clark

ALS. Dewey's shorthand note: "Clark, S. N. 76/7/17. About conference. Suggestions. Answered." Major S. N. Clark, one of the editors of the 1876 Report, and an assistant in the Bureau of Education.

[1]*John Eaton, U. S. Commissioner of Education.*

[2]*Reference to the prospectus of the* Library Journal, *which was included in* Public Libraries in the U. S., *1876, pp. xxvii-xxviii.*

57. *JOHN EATON TO DEWEY*

DEPARTMENT OF THE INTERIOR
Bureau of Education
Washington, D. C., July 15, 1876

Dear Sir:

Your favor respecting the sending out of the call for the librarians' convention by this office is received. It is entirely proper that it should be so sent. If you will send the printed copies to the Bureau by mail (I enclose postage stamps for the purpose) I will cause them to be addressed and sent to libraries with the least practicable delay. I should think that 2,000 copies of the call would be sufficient. A copy of the prospectus as revised by Mr. Leypoldt is inclosed as you request.[1]

Very respectfully
Your obedient Servant
John Eaton

LS. Dewey's shorthand note: "Eaton will send call from office. 76/7/17. answered."

[1]*Prospectus of* Library Journal. *See* Public Libraries in the U.S., *1876, pp. xxvii-xxviii.*

58. S. N. CLARK TO DEWEY

DEPARTMENT OF THE INTERIOR
Bureau of Education
Washington, D. C., July 15, 1876

Dear Sir:

Your favors are received. I have prepared a copy of the table of contents of the library report for your use.[1] Should you desire more particular information respecting any chapter please let me know. A copy of the prospectus of the Library Journal as revised by Mr. Leypoldt will be sent you today. It will appear in the report in about its present form unless you choose to condense it still further. It seems to us that the call might state the prospects of a fall meeting at Philadelphia and contain an urgent invitation to all librarians to attend, but you and Mr. Winsor will know best.

It may not be improper for Mr. Warren[2] and I to mention some matters which we should be glad to see presented for the consideration of the Convention. Briefly, they are as follows:

1. Library records, reports and statistics. What records should be kept in different classes of libraries? Is it practicable to secure uniformity of records and statistics? Can a uniform classification of books for the purpose of keeping a record of circulation be agreed upon? No comparison of statistics of use of different libraries will be of much value until some uniformity of classification is secured. Few libraries appear to keep account of net gain in books, or of losses showing proportions sold, worn out and lost. Is it practicable and, if so, is it worth while to classify readers and borrowers at public libraries? Most of the British free libraries try to do this, so far as to show the number of youths and adults—and some, the occupations of readers. Is it practicable to fix on some uniform plan of ennumerating unbound pamphlets, so that they can be properly added in making up an account of the strength of libraries? Is the volume the proper library unit? These are a few of the points that suggest themselves on the subject of statistics.

2. Library Financial Statements. Cannot some agreement be reached to enable a comparison of library finances? The lack of uniformity and completeness is nowhere more apparent than in this particular. A majority of the financial reports of libraries are far from being clear and understandable.

These two subjects present themselves most forcibly to us as the result of our experience in the work of gauging the strength, usefulness and resources of American libraries; though we are far ahead of any other country *now* in the matter of library statistics.

The subjects of pagination and sizes of books have been suggested by Mr. Thomas Hale Williams of the Minneapolis, (Minn.,) Athenæum,[3] and they have not been treated in the library report.

Yours very truly
S. N. Clark

P. S. The copyist has made a mistake in the prospectus and I will have to retain it until Monday.

ALS. Dewey's shorthand note: "Clark, S. N. About conference suggestions. Answered. 76/7/17."

[1]*Dewey included the table of contents and a review (from advance sheets) of* Public Libraries in the U. S., *1876, in the first issue of the* American Library Journal. ALJ, *1 (Sept. 30, 1876), 7-10.*

[2]*Samuel R. Warren, the other editor of* Public Libraries in the U.S., *1876, and an assistant in the Bureau of Education.*

[3]*Thomas Hale Williams to John Eaton, copy of letter [?] August 3, 1875, [?] Minneapolis Athenæum. See introduction, footnote 16.*

59. CUTTER TO WINSOR

BOSTON ATHENÆUM
Boston, July 24, 1876

Dear Sir

Do not give my paper any more particular title in your programme than "On the preservation of pamphlets."[1]

YT
C. A. Cutter

Postcard, signed. Although this is the only holograph item of Cutter, he undoubtedly exercised considerable influence on both Dewey and Winsor personally since they were in the same city and could see each other frequently.

[1]*Cutter, "The Preservation of Pamphlets,"* ALJ, *1* (*Nov. 30, 1876*), *51-54, 101-103.*

60. POOLE TO WINSOR

PUBLIC LIBRARY OF CHICAGO
Chicago, July 24, 1876

Dear Winsor

Yours of the 21st is rec'd.[1] The subjects you name for yourself. Smith and Cutter are good. I have not fixed on one yet. I am willing to take what the others do not take. The subject you mentioned to me in a previous letter—The Methods of Circulation—I have treated somewhat fully in my paper for Gen. Eaton,[2] and have given drawings of the apparatus we use. I don't think it would be well for me to repeat that matter, and that would be about what I should want to put into a paper. Something will turn up that will be the thing for me.

How many papers do you propose to have? "Five or ten minutes" is a very short time for a paper. You had better say *fifteen or twenty* and require everybody to stick to it. You could not on the subject you propose, say hardly anything in ten minutes. Perhaps you intend to have the subject brought out further in conversation after the paper is read.

Gen. Eaton's[3] will probably be out soon. I read my proof about two weeks ago. The paper had been in his hands more than a year.

The call for the Conference had better be issued soon. It will not be necessary in that call to publish a programme of exercises. The fact that the Conference will be held at the date fixed upon should be given to the public as early as possible, that librarians may bring it into their plans of summer vacations. But for this engagement I should be away this or the coming month.

Yours very truly
W. F. Poole

ALS.

[1]*Not located.*

[2]" *The Organization and Management of Libraries,*" *in* Public Libraries in the U.S., *1876, pp. 498-504 deal with circulation.*

[3]Ibid.

61. *PROPOSED LIBRARY CONVENTION AT PHILADELPHIA*

A convention of librarians is likely to be held in Philadelphia next October. The profession is awaking to a sense that it is a profession, and beginning to feel that it has as much need of and as much right to an organization as the teachers, or doctors, or dentists, or firemen. Conventions may not produce any very startling results; the papers read may be empty, or dull, or wrong-headed; the few valuable essays may find a tired or inattentive audience; but good-fellowship is likely to be promoted and *esprit de corps* increased, and, in the present case, something will be gained by the public recognition of the existence of the occupation, as one having certain special duties, requiring peculiar aptitudes, and deserving to be entered by an apprenticeship. As long as the chief libraries were those of colleges or historical societies, used by comparatively few readers, of whom a large part might be expected to be trained in investigation and the use of books, it was natural and not objectionable that librarianship should be a refuge for those who had failed in other occupations. With the growth, however, of city and mercantile libraries, dealing with large numbers of borrowers, where promptitude and despatch were all-important, a new class of men were secured—men having, if not business training, at least aptitude for business. And as the work possible to libraries has developed, and they have more and more come forward as companion educators to the public schools, it has further become evident that the man of business is not competent to do all that a librarian can do usefully. All librarians are more or less called on to assist investigation; if not supposed to be omniscient, they are at least expected to know where to look for any bit of information that is wanted. But the town librarian cannot be content with this; he must be qualified to direct the reading of his clientage; he should be in a way the literary pastor of the town; he must be able to become familiar with his flock, especially with the young, to gain their confidence, to select their reading, and gradually to elevate their taste. Like a minister, he must be content with slow progress and meagre results. It is only by flowery paths and gentle ascents that he can lead them from Braddon to Scott and from Tupper to Tennyson. But he will keep his object always in mind, and will never be satisfied but as he sees the percentage of fiction read decreasing and the proportion of travels, and history, and science, and philosophy increasing. There are librarians who have effected this, some by annotated catalogues, some by personal intercourse (that is, as it were, by the sermon and by the pastoral visit). If they can be brought together and made to tell their methods, others will be moved to imitate them. This, at least, was the result of the Convention of 1853 at New York—a meeting which has probably never been heard of by the greater part of the present generation of librarians. Frequent conventions may become wearisome, but one every twenty-three years can certainly be endured by the most indifferent of the profession.

Article written by Cutter for *The Nation*, 23 (July 27, 1876), 59-60.

62. *LIBRARY CONFERENCE (SECOND PRINTED CALL)*

LIBRARY CONFERENCE

THE Committee, to whom were intrusted the arrangements for the proposed Conference of Librarians and others interested in bibliography and library economy, have selected Philadelphia as the place of meeting, and Wednesday, Thursday, and Friday, October 4–6, as the date. The government of the Historical Society of that city have kindly offered their rooms for the purpose.

The proposed Conference receives the cordial support of many eminent librarians who have been consulted, among whom may be named:

CHARLES A. CUTTER, Boston Athenæum; J. L. WHITNEY, Boston Public Library; FRED. B. PERKINS, Boston Public Library; JOHN LANGDON SIBLEY, Harvard University Library; JOHN FISKE, Harvard University Library; EZRA ABBOT, Harvard University; S. F. HAVEN, American Antiquarian Society, Worcester; REUBEN A. GUILD, Brown University Library; J. D. HEDGE, Providence Athenæum; ADDISON VAN NAME, Yale College Library; FRANKLIN B. DEXTER, Yale College Library; A. S. PACKARD, Bowdoin College Library; J. CARSON BREVOORT,

Astor Library; F. SAUNDERS, Astor Library; W. S. BUTLER, New-York Society Library; W. T. PEOPLES, New-York Mercantile Library; JACOB SCHWARTZ, Apprentices' Library, New-York; S. B. NOYES, Brooklyn Mercantile Library; H. A. HOMES, New-York State Library; JAS. G. BARNWELL, Philadelphia Mercantile Library; JOHN EATON, Bureau of Education, Washington; CHAS. EVANS, Indianapolis Public Library; THOS. VICKERS, Cincinnati Public Library; JNO. N. DYER, St. Louis Mercantile Library.

The Committee are providing for papers and discussions which can not fail to be of interest to those attending the Conference, and plans for a permanent organization and other business will also be presented. A programme will be ready in September, which will be mailed by the Secretary *on application*.

There is promise of a large attendance of librarians and others interested in library work, and all will be cordially welcome.

JUSTIN WINSOR, *Boston Public Library*,

WM. F. POOLE, *Chicago Public Library*,

LLOYD P. SMITH, *Philadelphia Library Co.*,

COMMITTEE

MELVIL DEWEY, *Secretary*,

13 Tremont Place, Boston

------- ►◄◆►◄ -------

Document. American Antiquarian Society copy. Another copy of this call can be found in the Evans Papers, University of Illinois, but none exists in the scrapbook itself. This announcement was mailed to approximately 1,000 libraries and librarians on July 28, 1876 with more copies mailed the next day. See items 63 and 57. The call was also published in its entirety in *PW*, 10 (July 29, 1876), 204-205. Cutter had noted in his July 27 column in *The Nation*, item 61, the likelihood that the convention would take place, and confirmed it in his August 3 column. Probably encouraged by Dewey, the Boston *Advertiser* announced: "The library interest in this country is becoming so large, and questions of administrations and economy so numerous and important, that it has been decided to hold a general conference of librarians and others interested in bibliography at Philadelphia in October next. The meeting will be held at the rooms of the Pennsylvania Historical Society, and a permanent organization on the basis of a community of interests will undoubtedly be formed. The conference has the approval of most of the leading librarians in the country." Boston *Advertiser*, July 28, 1876, p. 2, col. 3. In New York City *The World*, July 31, 1876, p. 6, col. 2, printed the call, and it is likely that newspapers in other metropolitan areas did the same, although I have not checked. In similar language, the announcement was published in Great Britain in *Notes and Queries*, 5th series, VI (Aug. 19, 1876), 159-160. The same names appear on both printed calls but in slightly different order. During August, 1876, Dewey received 45 letters and postcards which are preserved in the scrapbook, but only eight are reproduced here since most of them were one or two-sentence requests for programs or conference information, or express regrets for inability to attend.

63. CLARK TO DEWEY

DEPARTMENT OF THE INTERIOR
Bureau of Education
Washington, D. C., July 28, 1876

Dear Sir

Your favor of yesterday is received.[1] We are losing no time in sending out the call. One thousand copies leave by tonight's mail; and the remainder tomorrow. Have telegraphed you for 500 additional copies which please send without delay to supply foreign demand and some other needs here. Do you wish any sent to publishers? We have as complete a list of foreign libraries as any one, I suppose.

I inclose you 20 three cent stamps. The proof you returned was delayed in the Washington office one day on account of non-payment of . . . .

AL. Only the first page preserved; second page missing. Dewey's shorthand at bottom of first page, after one illegible word, "S.N. Clark." On verso: "Clark, S. N. Sending call. Answering. 76/7/31."

[1] *Not located.*

64. SPOFFORD TO WINSOR

LIBRARY OF CONGRESS
Washington, Aug. 15th, 1876

Dear Sir:

In reply to your kind inquiry of 12th I will prepare a very brief paper on "Copyright in its relation to Libraries and Literature,"[1] for the October Convention of Librarians.

As I cannot be present during the whole term of the sittings I should like to have this assigned to one of the late sessions.

Very respectfully
A. R. Spofford
Librarian of Congress

ALS. Spofford did attend for just one day, Friday, October 6, 1876, where he read the above mentioned paper.

[1] *"Copyright in its Relation to Libraries and Literature,"* ALJ, *1 (Nov. 30, 1876), 84-89, 139.*

65. C. H. PLUGGÉ TO DEWEY

INTERNATIONAL EXHIBITION, 1876
UNITED STATES GOVERNMENT BUILDING
Department of the Interior Exhibit
Philadelphia, Aug. 28, 1876

Dear Sir:

If you send the invitations of which you speak in your letter of the 26th inst.[1] I'll forward them to American and foreign educators here.

Very respectfully yours
C. H. Pluggé

P.S. Gen. Eaton will not be here before the middle of next month.

———————

ALS. Dewey's shorthand response: "I mail you today copies of the call which you kindly offer to forward to educators who may be interested. If more are needed I will gladly send them or perhaps if all these were sent to those most likely to attend or to give the matter sufficient attention it would be sufficient." On verso: "Eaton per Pluggé. Will send calls to foreign educators. 76/8/30."

[1]*Not located.*

66. SAUNDERS TO DEWEY

412 ADELPHI ST. BROOKLYN
Aug. 28/76

My dear Sir,

I have the pleasure of acknowledging receipt of your favor of the 24th inst.[1] and beg to say in reply that while I feel very sensibly the kindness and compliment of your invitation, I am yet compelled to deny myself the pleasure of its acceptance, in consequence of pressing preoccupations. I enclose a copy of the Sketch of Amer. Libraries[2] should you wish to make any extracts from it for your Journal. Hoping to have the pleasure of meeting with you at the approaching convention at Philadelphia, I remain

Very truly and respy yours
F. Saunders

———————

ALS. Dewey's shorthand response: "Dear Sir: I beg to acknowledge the receipt of your article. I regret that you are unable to prepare a paper for us at Philadelphia. We shall be very glad always to give place to anything you may write bearing on the library interest and of course shall reach a larger number of libraries than any other journal." On verso: "Saunders, Frederick, 8, 28, '6 Declining to prepare a paper for conference."

¹*Not located.*
²*No indication it was used in* LJ.

67. *THOMAS H. ROGERS TO WINSOR*

MONMOUTH, ILL.
Aug. 28, '76

Dear Sir,

I am exceedingly thankful that you have set on foot the idea of combined work in Library matters, and I look to the coming Convention at Phil. for much help and advantage to us all.

I hope that a very full report of the Convention, its discussions, reports, papers, &c will be published. Otherwise much of the benefit, it ought to bring, will be lost.

Allow me to suggest for your consideration a matter that it seems to me ought to be set on foot. There is need all over the country of a Library Index. A large number of the volumes of Essays, bound magazines, Collections &c are of course to be found in every considerable Library. If an Index of Subjects was printed for a large collection of such books (such a collection as your Library contains) it would cover all of such works in every small Library. If blanks were left where the catalogue number of such books could be inserted by each Library that would show which volumes it possessed. If some mark could be used to designate the same thing it would perhaps be best to bind it interleaved, or in scrap book fashion. There would be need to publish an Annual on the same plan indexing new volumes of essays, collections, leading magazines &c.

I think every Public Library would subscribe for such a work and that the publishers would also subscribe largely for it. Not one Library in ten can do for itself this kind of work. A vast number of books would be used if this was done which now are idle in all the smaller libraries of the country.

We find our bound magazines are in constant use since we began to publish lists of continued articles and stories contained in them.

Please to consider this matter if you think it worth while. The Public Libraries owe you a debt of gratitude for what you have done for them all.

With highest respect I am

Thankfully yours
Thomas H. Rogers
Secy W. Co. Lby

ALS. Dewey's shorthand reply on verso (partly illegible) "For the October conference receive from you a paper in your letter so please ..." At top: "Rogers, Thomas H. Conference Answered 31." Thomas H. Rogers (1836-1914), charter member, Board of Trustees, Warren County Library, and for over 30 years Secretary of the Board.

68. S. B. NOYES TO DEWEY

MER. LIBRARY, BROOKLYN
30 Aug., 1876

Dear Sir.

I wish I could see my way toward complying with your kind invitation, but I am so hard pushed by library & catalogue work that I can't concentrate my thoughts on any special topic outside of my daily task, and if I go to Phila., which I hope to do, it must be as a listener. Much of the catalogue I have to manufacture as I go along, and at this season of the year I don't find much energy left even for the arrears of library work which have accumulated.

I am very glad there is such promise of a successful conference, but please omit me from your list of *specials*.

Yours very truly
S. B. Noyes

ALS. Dewey's shorthand response: "I am ever so sorry that you can't give us anything. Don't, on any account, fail of being at the meeting in October. By the way, can't you send something for the first number of the JOURNAL? It will go to all the libraries of this country as a prospectus and specimen, and you will hardly have another chance to reach so large an audience of librarians. I wish you might send something that will serve as a text for the Philadelphia discussions."

For a review of Noyes' alphabetico-classed catalog see ALJ, 1 (May 31, 1877), 330-331.

69. GREEN TO DEWEY

FREE PUBLIC LIBRARY
Worcester, Mass. Aug. 31, 1876

Dear Sir,

I received your letter yesterday.[1]

Excuse me for not answering last evening. I was surprised, but certainly very much gratified, to be invited to prepare a paper for the conference.

In thinking the matter over I find that I have some thoughts which I should like to present to the body of librarians and which would naturally arrange themselves under the following head:

The desirableness of establishing personal
intercourse and relations between librarians
and readers in popular libraries.[2]

You will notify me in good time, I presume what limits should be observed in the time to be occupied in reading the paper?

truly yours
Samuel S. Green

ALS. Dewey's shorthand on verso: "Green, S. S. Will furnish paper. 9/1."

[1] *Not located, but presumably similar to the invitations to Evans and Haven. See items 72 and 73.*

[2] "*Personal Relations between Librarians and Readers,*" ALJ, *1* (*Nov. 30, 1876*), *74-81, 123-124.*

70. HOMES TO DEWEY

Dear Sir,

In part and as a preliminary answer to your note of ————,[1] I mailed to you to day two pamphlets, which will form part of the Washington Bureau of Education's forthcoming volume on Libraries.[2] From these, you will see that I have already expressed all I have to say, in two directions at least. I thank you for your invitation to say more on some other topics, in case I should find it possible to be present in Philadelphia. I think I ought to have indulged the purpose for several months, in order to allow the fitting material to crystallize about a nucleus; and do not dare to engage that I should venture to contribute any thing.

I think if I should attempt any thing, I ought to be able to say something practical on the Arrangement of Subject Indexes: and as my mind is at present I will keep that topic before me during the month.[3] If I am not able to be present, it will be my chief regret to fail to meet so many with whom after long years of service one feels a cordial fellowship from similarity of pursuits.

Very sincerely yours
Henry A. Homes

ALS. Dewey's shorthand response: "We will put the arrangement of subject headings on our program against your name and hope you may be present. If that can not be we shall hope for a communication on the subject which some of us can read. I really hope you may be present as there is promise of an excellent meeting."

[1]*Not located but presumably similar to the invitations to Evans and Haven. See items 72 and 73.*

[2]*Probably* Historical Societies in the United States, *14 p., reprinted from* Public Libraries in the U.S., *1876, pp. 312-325, and possibly* "State and Territorial Libraries," Public Libraries in the U. S., *1876, pp. 292-311.*

[3]*Homes' paper did not appear on the programme, but was read in place of that of S. F. Haven. Homes, "Subject Indexes," ALJ, 1 (Nov. 30, 1876), 81-84, 90, 129.*

71. PLUGGÉ TO DEWEY

INTERNATIONAL EXHIBITION, 1876
UNITED STATES GOVERNMENT BUILDING
Department of the Interior Exhibit
Philadelphia, Aug. 31, 1876

Dear Sir:

The invitations you kindly sent me to-day for distribution have been forwarded to foreign and American educators and other persons interested in education. Several foreign gentlemen have promised me to attend the Conferences. I kept some copies for persons who are expected from Europe during September.

Very respectfully
Your ob't. servant
C. H. Pluggé

ALS. Dewey's shorthand response: "Many thanks. The interest you have manifested in our work will certainly be appreciated by the librarians of the country who, I assure you, will know of that work."

The Call Sent Far and Wide—
with Dewey's Shorthand Thanks

JOHN EATON,
*Representative of the Department
of the Interior.*

INTERNATIONAL EXHIBITION, 1876.

UNITED STATES GOVERNMENT BUILDING,

Department of the Interior Exhibit.

Philadelphia, Aug 31 1876.

Dear Sir:

The invitations you
Kindly sent me to-day
for distribution have been
forwarded to foreign and
American educators and
other persons interested
in education. Several
foreign gentlemen have
promised me to attend
the Conferences. I Kept
some copies for persons
who are expected from
Europe during September,

Very respectfully
Your obt. Servant
C. H. Penzzé

Melvil Dewey Esq.
Boston.

72. DEWEY TO EVANS

[BOSTON, AUGUST, 1876]

Dear Sir:

The com. of arrangements for the coming conference would be pleased to have you prepare for that occasion a paper on some subject pertaining to libraries or librarians. The program already contains the names of Spofford, Winsor, Cutter, Poole, Smith & others. Will you kindly advise us of the topic on which you will write? As we are about sending to press the program for distribution thru the country, an early reply will greatly oblige us.

Very truly

Melvil Dewey

ALS. Evans Papers, IUL. Written on verso of the July printed call for a conference and dated in Evans' handwriting, "Melvil Dewey, Boston, Mass., Sept. 1876." Apparently all the invitations to prospective speakers were written on the verso of the conference call. S. S. Green and H. A. Homes received their invitations to speak, respectively on August 30 and 31, so the Evans and Haven invitations were probably written the last week in August, even though both recipients dated them "Sept., 1876." Most probable date of writing: August 29, 1876. See Evans' letter of September 15 (item 86) accepting Dewey's invitation. Evans had been on vacation and his acceptance did not reach Dewey in time to be included on the printed program (advance proof). It was included in the ALJ itself, however. On September 25 Poole wrote Evans encouraging him to be present at the conference, apparently not knowing that Evans had already accepted the invitation to deliver a paper (item 92). One might remark that the last week in August is rather late to be asking for a paper for an October 4 conference!

73. DEWEY TO HAVEN

[BOSTON, AUGUST, 1876]

Dear Sir:

The committee of arrangements for the approaching conference of librarians would be pleased to have you prepare for that occasion a paper on some subject pertaining to libraries or librarians. Will you kindly inform the sec. of the committee on what topic you will write? We should like this at your earliest convenience for we are about sending to press the program for distribution thro'out the country, and should like your subject sent in time to be included in that program. Papers are already on the program from Spofford, Winsor, Cutter, Poole, Smith and others. An early reply will oblige us greatly as we wish to print the program at the earliest practicable moment.

Very truly
Melvil Dewey

I ought to add that we are daily receiving letters from persons interested who are to be present at the meeting, and everything promises to be even more profitable and enjoyable than we had at first anticipated.

ALS, on verso of second printed call. AAS. Dated in another hand "Sept. 1876," but probably sent out at the same time as those to Green and Homes. Most probable date is August 29, 1876. Haven first accepted (item 74), but later had to decline (item 98).

74. HAVEN TO DEWEY

AMERICAN ANTIQUARIAN SOCIETY
Worcester, Mass. Sept. 1, 1876

Dear Sir,

I have been quite at a loss to meet the request that I should prepare a paper for the meeting of Librarians. It happens, however, that just now I am engaged on plans for the enlargement of our library building, and perhaps I may have some thoughts to express on Library Construction.

As this topic pertains to the general subject proposed to me "Libraries or Librarians" I think I will adopt it.

The modes of construction appropriate to Public Libraries[1]

Yours very truly
S. F. Haven

ALS. Dewey's shorthand response on verso: "Haven 9,1, '6 To speak on bldgs. library paper Answered:

Dear Sir

I recorded you on the program for the topic suggested which I am sure will be of interest for it is eminently a practical question.

We hope we shall hear from you often thru the columns of our journal. The first number goes to all of the librarians of the country and largely abroad reaching nearly all of the librarians of the world.

If you have something that you would like to say to such an unusual audience send it to me by the 10th of the month. It's a rare opportunity to stimulate thought on library lines and I really hope you will improve it."

Dewey's formal response, identical with this shorthand version, dated Sept. 2, 1876, is in AAS.

[1]*Haven later could not attend and sent Edmund Mills Barton (1838-1918) Assistant Librarian, American Antiquarian Society, 1866-1883, in his place. The proposed paper did not materialize.* ALJ, 1 (*Nov. 30, 1876*), 90.

75. SCHWARTZ TO DEWEY

Dear Sir

I take the earliest opportunity I can to write a few lines in relation to your last favor.[1]

I regret that I cannot give you any definite promise as to a paper for the Conference, first because the time allowed is rather short and secondly because your invitation is too general. What kind of paper would be in order? Can you without violating any confidence inform me of the topics treated of in the papers of Messrs. Cutter, Winsor &c? How *long* a paper is expected? Again I do not know that I am competent to write anything worthy of the attention of the Conference. The only topic in Library Economy that I can lay any particular claim to know even partially is that of the arrangement and notation of books on the shelves. Would a paper [on] *my* scheme be appropriate?[2]

The change of date from Augt. to Oct. will make it somewhat difficult for me to be present as the latter date falls in our busiest part of the season, and I shall besides be then occupied in preparing my Annual Report, which altho occupying but a few pages, represents several weeks of very hard labor.

> An early answer will oblige
> Yours very truly
> Jacob Schwartz
> Librarian

ALS. Notation at the side says "I think this would do," and at bottom, "No harm in telling him what other papers are on. 10 or 15 minutes is enough." These notations are probably from Justin Winsor. Also at the bottom "I send a communication for the 1st no. of Lib. J1."

Dewey's shorthand note: "Hand this to Winsor and ask him what reply to make [to] J.W.S." On verso: "My dear Mr. Schwartz: The other papers are about 10-15 minutes long.

Winsor	On helps to readers
Cutter	Pamphlets
Smith	Qualifications of a librarian
Spofford	Copyright in its relations to libraries and literature
Holmes [sic]	Arrangement of indexes
Green (Worcester)	Personal intercourse between librarians and readers
Haven	Modes of construction for library buildings

Poole and others have not yet announced their subjects. You will of course select your own subject. Your scheme would be perfectly appropriate. We expect to have the Washington report in the hands of the convention so you would hardly want to duplicate any part of that I suppose. Can't you send in something for the first number of the Journal which goes to press in about a week? We shall send it to all the libraries and you will reach a big audience with anything you may give us for that number. We shall hope to hear from you often in our columns." Jacob Schwartz (1846-1918?), Librarian, New York Apprentices' Library, 1873-1900.

[1]*Not located, but presumably similar to the invitations to Haven and Evans. See items 72 and 73.*

[2]*Schwartz wrote on his classification scheme for the government report, hence Dewey's admonition. Jacob A. Schwartz, "New York Apprentices' Library Catalogue,"* Public Libraries in the U.S., *1876, pp. 657-660. He did not send anything for the first number of ALJ.*

76. BARNWELL TO DEWEY

Philadelphia Sept. 4th 1876

Dear Sir:-

Your favor (without date) endorsed on the Circular concerning the "Library Conference" has been duly received.[1]

Should my business engagements permit me to be in Philadelphia at the time of the Conference I expect to have ready a paper on "A Universal Catalogue: its necessity and practicability."[2]

Should my name be on the programme, please be careful that I am not designated as "Librarian" of this Institution. Though I have been both a professional and amateur Librarian, my present connection with the Mercantile is simply that of a Member of the Board and Chairman of the Committee.

Very truly
James G. Barnwell

A copy of the Programme is requested.

———————

ALS. Dewey's shorthand response on verso: "You have chosen a happy subject for the Conference, one that ought to be treated, and no one else has chosen it. We shall hope to hear from you often thru columns of this Journal." Although the librarian, John Edmands, was present, Barnwell was a far more active participant on behalf of the Mercantile Library.

[1]*Not located, but presumably similar to the invitations to Evans and Haven. See items 72 and 73.*

[2]*"A Universal Catalogue: Its Necessity and Practicability,"* ALJ, *1 (Nov. 30, 1876), 54-58, 106.*

77. S. S. GREEN TO THE EDITOR OF THE LIBRARY JOURNAL

Worcester Free Public Library
Sept. 4, 1876

To the Editor of the Library Journal:

It would add greatly to the usefulness of our reference libraries if an agreement should be made to lend books to each other for short periods of time. It happens not unfrequently that some book is called for by a reader, or that in looking up the answer to a question a librarian has occasion to use a book which he finds in the catalogue of another library, but which does not belong in his own collection. The book, very likely, is one that can be replaced if lost. But it would take time to get it through ordinary channels; it might be necessary to send abroad for a copy or to wait to pick up one, if the book is scarce. In such a case it would be a great convenience to be able to borrow a book for a few days.

The Boston Public Library allows students in special branches of knowledge, when properly introduced, to take out books needed in the pursuit of their special investigations, even although they do not live in Boston.

If libraries were to agree to help one another in this way, much good would result.

Perhaps those libraries which now allow books to be taken out by certain classes of non-residents would like to have applicants introduced through the libraries of the towns where they live, and instead of sending books to individuals, would prefer to send them to libraries to be delivered by them to applicants, and to be looked after as they look after their own books.

There would be a certain increase in the sense of safety in the consciousness that a library knows the peculiarities of its own readers better than they can be known to the officers of a distant institution.

I should think libraries would be willing to make themselves responsible for the value of the borrowed books, and be willing to pay an amount of expressage that would make the transportation company liable for the loss in money should the books disappear in transit.

Is not some such plan as the one suggested practicable?

I am informed that a plan of this kind is in operation in Europe, and that in many places it is easy to get through the local library books belonging to libraries in distant countries. If I am correctly informed, valuable books and even manuscripts are thus sent from one library to another to a very considerable extent.

Reference libraries, it is true, all have exceptionally valuable books that they would not be willing to lend. All, too, have books that by the conditions of the gift can not be allowed outside of the building of the library which owns them. This condition is annexed to so many of the books in the reference department of the Worcester Library that I hesitate in urging the plan recommended. We have no printed catalogue either, of the reference department.

But even if for these reasons the privilege desired could not be extended to the library under my charge, why should not such libraries as can assist each other whenever in their power to do so?

I do not propose a definitely-formed plan for carrying out the recommendation contained in this letter, but only ask librarians and others to consider whether it would not be well to form one, and whether it is not feasible to make one.

Perhaps the matter is worthy the consideration of the Conference of Librarians at Philadelphia.

Samuel S. Green

Printed letter, ALJ, 1 (Sept. 30, 1876), 15-16. Green's suggestions on interlibrary lending did not form the basis for either a paper or for a discussion at the conference.

78. GUILD TO DEWEY

LIBRARY OF BROWN UNIVERSITY
Providence, R.I., Sept. 4, 1876

Dear Sir.

Your communication respecting Conference of Librarians came duly to hand but at a late day.[1] The truth is I have been stopping with my family during the Summer on the Conanicut Island, opposite Newport, where mail facilities are not the best. In consequence of the long continued sickness during the past Winter of my oldest son, and his final death, I had become worn down and exhausted with grief and fatigue and needed *rest*. I now feel prepared for another year's work.

In regard to a paper for the Conference. As you have kindly allowed me to select a Subject I will take

"Bibliography as a Science"[2]

and endeavor in a few hours snatched from conflicting duties and cares to do something for the occasion. Having treated this Subject already in my "Librarian's Manual"[3] I shall of course feel better prepared to write on it than I should on another theme.

It is possible that I may not be able to meet you in Phila. on the 4th 5 & 6. Our term opens Sept. 20. The Library which is large (50,000 vols) is much used by the 300 Students & 15 Professors. It is open every day from 10 till 3, and I have no assistant. To close up for a week at the beginning of the term would be a serious matter, and to leave the Library in charge of an inexperienced person would also be a serious matter. I will at all events do the best I can.

If convenient please drop me a line in reply. I shall return from the Island next week and resume work as usual.

In haste
Yours fraternally & truly
Reuben A. Guild

———————◄-◄●●►-◄———————

ALS. Dewey's shorthand reply on verso: "Dear Sir: Your letter is just at hand. Your subject is fortunate as no one else has chosen anything like it. I have included it in the program.

It would be quite too bad if you should be prevented from coming to Philadelphia with us. You could leave Tuesday night after closing and get back to open Saturday morning and still attend all our meetings. That is, you would have to leave someone else only three days. I have at Amherst twenty-two assistants from the students and so have not the slightest difficulty in leaving at any time. Of course they have to be kept on leading strings.

We send our first number of the LIBRARY JOURNAL to press the 15th and it will go to all the libraries of the country. If you could send us anything before that time, it would reach a larger audience than again for years.[4] I hope you may send something if it be only a brief communication, for it's a rare chance to reach our library interest in all sections."

[1]*Not located, but presumably similar to the invitations to Evans and Haven. See items 72 and 73.*

[2]*"Bibliography as a Science,"* ALJ, *1 (Nov. 30, 1876), 67-69.*

[3]The Librarian's Manual; a Treatise on Bibliography . . . (*New York: C. B. Norton, 1858), 304 p.*

[4]*Guild did submit a paragraph on the new library of Brown University,* ALJ, (*Sept. 30, 1876), 25.*

79. THOMAS H. ROGERS TO DEWEY

MONMOUTH, ILL.

Sept. 7th, 76

Dear Sir,

Please to thank the Committee for their kind request for a paper from me for the Library Conference.

I shall be glad to do what I can for the good cause. My time is so taken up that I can only furnish a short paper. The subject is one that has interested me for years. You may state the title as "A Cooperative Index for Public Libraries."[1]

I have been prevented by sickness in my family from writing you sooner. By what date should the paper be sent you?

Yours truly
Thos H. Rogers
Superintendent
Warren Co. Library

ALS. Rogers was unable to attend the conference, and William E. Foster read his paper for him. Rogers' paper occasioned a lengthy discussion regarding indexing and particularly the continuation of Poole's index.

[1] *"A Co-operative Index,"* ALJ, *1 (Nov. 30, 1876), 62-63, 112-117.*

80. SMITH TO WINSOR

LIBRARY CO. OF PHILADA

Philadelphia, Sept. 9, 1876

My dear Sir,

I have written at length to Mr. Dewey[1] & requested him to show the letter & its enclosures to you.

To enable the Committee to consult to advantage & also to give me he pleasure of a visit from you & the others I want you, Mr. Poole & Mr. Dewey to make my house your home during the Convention. My resi- lence is No. 2 Shoemaker Lane, Germantown. In coming from Boston lo not go on to the Station in West Phila. but stop at Intersection & ake the Germantown cars to Shoemaker Lane. I should be glad to see you] either Saturday, Sunday or Monday as may suit your conven- ence, & will meet you if possible at Germantown Intersection.

I shall extend a similar invitation to Mr. Poole by this mail.[2]

Yours very truly
Lloyd P. Smith

ALS.

[1] *Item 81.*
[2] *Not located, but see Poole to Winsor, item 89.*

81. *SMITH TO DEWEY*

Sep 9 1876

PRIVATE

My dear Sir,

In reply to your postal card[1] I enclose a letter which you print in No. 1 of the Journal if you think proper.[2]

You have not let me know the result of your inquiries after a suitable Hotel for the members of the Convention. Enclosed is a letter from Mr. Poole partly on that subject which I beg you will answer.[3] If you have not selected a Hotel I shall name the Hotel Aubry to any that apply.

However I wish you, Mr. Poole & Mr. Winsor to stay at my house during the sitting of the Convention & you had all better get there by Saturday or Monday previous. I live at No. 2 Shoemakers' Lane, Germantown. In coming from Boston stop at Germantown Intersection & take the Germantown Railroad to Shoemakers Lane. If you will let me know when you arrive at Intersection I will try & meet you. All being together we can arrange the Programme which need not be announced until the morning of the 4th. I propose that we meet at 10 o'clock at the Historical Society. In the afternoon of that day go to the Ridgway Building & in the evening there will be a reception with a collation as an act of hospitality on the part of the Philadelphia Librarians.

I have prepared a short paper on the *Qualifications of Librarians*[4] which I will read if there is time & on which I would like to hear a discussion by the members.

Yours very truly
Lloyd P. Smith

Please show this with the enclosures to Mr. Winsor

———————•◦•◦•◦——————

ALS. Dewey's shorthand notes: "Smith, L. P. 76/9/9 Answered." For a description of the meeting at Smith's house see Samuel S. Green, *Public Library Movement*, pp. 17-18.

[1]*Not located.*

[2]*See printed letter with advance proof of the program, item 93.*

[3]*Not located.*

[4]"*The Qualifications of a Librarian*," ALJ, *1 (Nov. 30, 1876), 69-74. Smith's paper apparently occasioned no discussion.*

2. *JAMES YATES TO DEWEY*

LEEDS PUBLIC LIBRARY, ENGLAND
September 9th, 1876

Dear Sir,

I have great pleasure in accepting your kind invitation to attend the Librarians' Conference in Philadelphia.

I shall arrive in New York by the S. S. 'Wyoming,' Union Line, about the 23rd inst. and intend calling upon Mr. W. S. Butler, New York Society Library; and shall feel obliged by your kindly forwarding me a Programme to that address, to enable me to ascertain the manner in which I may be most helpful to my Confrères.

I remain

Yours respectfully,
James Yates

ALS. James Yates (1843-1913), Librarian, Leeds Public Library, 1870-1897. Dewey's shorthand note on verso: "Dear Sir: Your letter reached me in this mail. I answer at once as I fear I may fail to reach you in care of Mr. Butler of New York on whom, you write me, you are to call. We shall be most happy to welcome you to our meeting and shall depend on you for information on English libraries and methods. If possible we should be exceedingly glad to have you read a paper during our sessions. Hoping to have the honor of your acquaintance at an early date. I am." Yates participated actively in the conference, "made himself much liked, and was frequently and usefully called upon for English experience or English views." ALJ, 1 (Nov. 30, 1876), 90.

83. SCHWARTZ TO DEWEY

Dear Sir

I have delayed replying to your last favor until now,[1] as I have been very busy superintending the reopening of the library. I should very much like to contribute a paper to be read before the Convention but I am afraid I cannot find time. Our library force is very limited and a. we had a circulation of 150,000 vols. last year & over 7400 readers you can easily imagine that myself and five assistants (two of them under 16) had our hands full and as the present season promises to be ever more successful than the last, there will be little time left for anything but the routine work; I find also that enough work is laid out for me in addition to the routine work to keep me hard at work every spare moment until January next. In fact I have so little time at my own disposal that I have postponed my pamphlet on library Economy to the Greek Kalends.—

Should such a contingency arise, as a few spare hours, I shall perhaps write something but is altogether uncertain.

I had overlooked some important work to be done when I last wrote,[2] otherwise I could have informed you then of my inability to supply anything for the Convention.

Respectfully,
J. Schwartz

ALS. Dewey's shorthand note: "Schwartz, J. 76/9/10 answered." Schwartz did attend but did not take a prominent part in the discussions.

[1] *Original not located, but see the shorthand response of Dewey, on item 75.*
[2] *Item 75.*

LIBRARY C.° PHILADEL.ᴬ
Philadelphia, September 13, 1876

My dear Sir

I recd an acceptance¹ this morning from Mr. Poole of my invitation to stay with me during his visit & he thinks we ought all to come together at my house on Monday evening Oct. 2. I think so too.

I thought when I wrote you last that we met on a Tuesday and therefore named Tuesday afternoon for a visit to the Ridgway Library Building. I should have said Wednesday.²

I should like to know as soon as possible your estimate of the no. of delegates who will be present. I had a conference with the Librarian of the Historical Society³ this morning & he says the possibility of our having a reception & collation some evening will depend upon the no. to be present. Their rooms are not very capacious. If not too late any public notice of a Reception had better be omitted for the present.

I trust you & Mr. Winsor will be able to reach Germantown on Monday.

Yours very truly
Lloyd P. Smith

ALS. Dewey's shorthand reply: "My dear Mr. Smith. I shall try to be with you on Monday. Your mistake as to Tuesday being the 4th was corrected. I think we shall have over 100 people at our conferences, still it is wholly guess work.⁴ The cat is out of the bag for someone has put in the Boston papers⁵ that there will probably be an entertainment. As we shall have an evening session anyway, I think we had best let it go, nothing being said about the collation."

¹Not located.

²Tuesday, Oct. 4th, went out in the advance proof program but was corrected in ALJ itself.

[3]*John Jordan, Jr. (1808-1890), a Vice President, Historical Society of Pennsylvania, 1876-1890, also served as acting librarian in 1876.*

[4]*Actual attendance was 103.*

[5]*"National Library Conference,"* Boston Daily Advertiser, *Sept. 14, 1876, p. 1, col. 4.*

85. SMITH TO DEWEY

LIBRARY C°. PHILADEL.ª
Philadelphia, Sept. 15, 1876

My dear sir

Yours of 12 is at hand.[1]

I can do nothing better than the La Pierre,[2] which is every way a good selection.

I am glad you & Mr. Winsor will stay with me. Mr. Poole expects to arrive on Monday. Try & let me know at what hour you arrive Germantown Intersection on Tuesday.

I enclose a letter which I beg you will do with what you think best.[3]

Yours very truly
Lloyd P. Smith

ALS.

[1]*Not located.*

[2]*According to the ALJ, 1 (Sept. 30, 1876), 3, Dewey had managed to secure special rates at the Hotel Lafayette and La Pierre House, adjoining each other on Broad (14th) and Chestnut streets, with the latter being the cheaper hotel. These two hotels were selected as "headquarters," although from the busy three days it seems unlikely that anyone spent much time there. Dewey reported that, "no one desired to go to the Exposition so long as this valuable opportunity was before them, and so the Conference drove, drove, drove for three days," ALJ 1 (Nov. 30, 1876), 90. In the scrapbook are letters from the United States and Belmont hotels, but not from the Lafayette and La Pierre.*

[3]*This may be a reference to the letter of the proprietor of the Belmont Hotel, Sept. 11, 1876, to Dewey, calling attention to the hotel's facilities.*

6. EVANS TO DEWEY

PUBLIC LIBRARY
Indianapolis, Sept. 15, 1876

Dear Sir:

Just returning from a flying trip to the East,[1] where I endeavored to
see you, I find your undated note[2] asking me to prepare a paper for the
Oct. meeting of the Librarian's Convention.

Mr. Poole had previously written to me upon the same subject,[3] but
without receiving my reply. I will write to him, that I have promised
you, to call out discussion, if possible, upon the subject of "The sizes of
printed books."[4]

Very truly yours,
Charles Evans

ALS. Dewey's shorthand reply at top: "An excellent subject in which I
am especially interested. Thanks. I shall send you the first number of
the Journal this week I think." Recipient's copy, a postcard dated Sept.
20, 1876, in Evans Papers, IUL.

[1]*Evans took his vacation in the Boston area in late August.*
[2]*Item 72.*
[3]*Not located, but see item 92.*
[4]*"The Sizes of Printed Books," ALJ, 1 (Nov. 30, 1876), 58-61, 106-109,
139-140.*

87. LIBRARY AND BIBLIOGRAPHICAL NOTES

The Library Conference at Philadelphia promises to be very largely at tended; delegates from abroad, as well as American librarians, will be present. Several of the leading American authorities will read paper to open discussions on important topics. The first number of the *American Library Journal* will be ready the latter part of this month, with the full programme, papers from Mr. Winsor, Mr. Cutter, etc. The price will be $5 *per annum*, and subscriptions are now desired. They should be addressed to American Library Journal, 37 Park Row; inquiries as to the Conference or the *Journal* will be answered by Mr. Melvil Dewey 13 Tremont Street, Boston.

Article in *Publishers' Weekly*, 10 (September 16, 1876), 476. The Boston *Daily Advertiser*, Sept. 14, 1876, p. 1, col. 4, contained a three-paragraph announcement in which it remarked "The sessions of the Conference are to be held at the Pennsylvania Historical Society's rooms, at which an elegant entertainment is expected to be tendered ... by the library company." The *Advertiser*'s account is a great piece of publicity but its facts are considerably exaggerated.

88. POOLE TO DEWEY

CHICAGO PUBLIC LIBRARY, Sept. 18, 1876

I think you had better not make any arrangement for a short-hand report at present, and not without the full approval of the Conference. If it be thought best when we get together, a reporter can be engaged at an hour's notice. The expenses of the Conference must be kept down till we know how they are to be met. We cannot lay this upon the Librarians who attend.

W. F. Poole

Postcard, signed. The scrapbook contains a postcard of Smith to Dewey dated Sept. 18, 1876, stating "I quite agree to having a short-hand report of our sessions & beg you to arrange for it," but Poole's view prevailed. Poole's insistence that there not be a stenographer caused a heavy load to fall upon the three conference secretaries, Dewey, Evans, and Guild. Dewey called attention to this fact in his report, *ALJ*, 1 (Nov. 30, 1876), 91. See also Dewey to Bowker, ALS, Oct. 24, 1876, Bowker Papers, NYPL.

89. POOLE TO WINSOR

PUBLIC LIBRARY OF CHICAGO
Chicago, Sept. 18, 1876

My dear Winsor:

Yours of the 13th rec'd.[1] Glad you have accepted Smith's invitation. I shall be there Monday. I don't care about seeing programme if it is satisfactory to you. Dewey needs looking after or he will pile up expenses, so that they will be a burden to the librarians who are present. I don't think he ought to be allowed to incur any expense that is not authorized by the Committee or by you as representing it. I have a postal card today from him wanting to employ a short-hand reporter to make full reports of the Conference.[2] I have written to him to do nothing about it for the present.[3] That can be settled after we get together. If it should be thought best, a reporter could be engaged at an hour's notice.

I am somewhat in doubt whether we want full reports. It will be a premium offered to loquaciousness. And who is to bear the expense? Our librarians cannot do it. Please apply a breeching to Dewey & hold him back.

It is a pity that Gen. Eaton's book[4] will not be distributed before the Conference meets.

Yours truly
W. F. Poole

P. S. Fletcher writes to me that he can not be present at Phil. because his chief, J.H.T.[5] does not want the Library represented. Has J.H.T.'s corns been trodden on? What is the matter? Fletcher intended to go, and is much disappointed because he cannot.

W.F.P.

ALS. Superintendent's File, BPL. Poole's concern with expenses was a legitimate one. He wrote Winsor on July 7 that his staff had not had their salaries paid for three months because of the stringency of Chicago's finances (item 54). The pinch of the recession, which began in November, 1873, was being felt in other places besides Chicago. *Cf.* my *Charles Evans, American Bibliographer* (Urbana: Univ. of Illinois Press, 1963), pp. 59-61.

[1] *Not located.*

[2] *Not located.*

[3] *Item 88.*

[4] Public Libraries in the U.S., *1876. Warren arrived in Philadelphia on Thursday morning, October 5, with working copies of the report for the use of the conference.*

[5] *James Hammond Trumbull (1821-1897), Librarian, Watkinson Library, Hartford, Conn., 1866-1890.*

90. *SMITH TO WINSOR*

Sept. 18, 1876

I suggested to John William Wallace, Esq., President of the Historical Society, that a few words of welcome from him on the assembling of the convention would be proper, & he has kindly consented to utter them, provided it meets with your approbation. J. W. Wallace is also Librarian of our Law Library & the Reporter of the U. S. Supreme Court.

Lloyd P. Smith

Postcard, signed. Along side is written "How ans?" and Winsor's "*by all means* JW." John William Wallace (1815-1884) President of the Historical Society of Pennsylvania, 1868-1884, delivered an excellent speech, summing up the problems of libraries, their growth, and necessity of bibliographical control of publications. ALJ, 1 (Nov. 30, 1876), 92-95. The address was also printed separately for the use of the conference. ALJ, 1 (Nov. 30, 1876), 104, and a copy has been located at the Library of Congress. G. K. Hall Co. reprinted this speech in 1965.

91. *ANNIE R. GODFREY TO DEWEY*

WELLESLEY, Sept. 19, '76

Dear Sir,

I notice in the "Call for Lib. Conf."[1] it is stated that it will *probably* be held in Mercantile Hall Oct. 4-6th. Some one from the Athenæum told me today they understood it was from 2d to 4th.

I leave here on Sat. for Phila. and hope to remain to attend it. If any change has been or is to be made will you please send me a line, either here or 1622 Chestnut St. Phila. care Mrs. Amos Leland. Also the house if known.

The paper came Sat. eve.[2]

Miss Clarke[3] from the Athenæum will take my place during my absence and has already commenced on the shelf lists. We should have been glad to have had your advice but had to make a beginning the best way we could.

Hastily
A. R. Godfrey

ALS. Annie R. Godfrey (1850-1922), Librarian, Wellesley College, 1875-1878, and one of the 13 women to attend the conference. She married Melvil Dewey on October 19, 1878.

[1] *Where Miss Godfrey received her information about the location of the Mercantile Library is uncertain, but it may have come from a misinterpretation of Lloyd P. Smith's letter of Sept. 9, 1876, published with the program (item 93). However, that program clearly states that "The Conference of Librarians will assemble at the rooms of the Pennsylvania Historical Society."*

[2] *Uncertain reference.*

[3] *Probably Emma Leonore Clarke, Boston Athenæum staff member, 1869-1890.*

92. POOLE TO EVANS

y

PUBLIC LIBRARY OF CHICAGO
Chicago, September 25, 1876

My dear Mr. Evans

Your letter of the 23d is rec'd.[1] While glad to hear from you I am sorry to infer, though you do not say so, that you will not be present at the Phil. Conference. I wish you would so arrange it as to be there. My board voted me two weeks absence for this business. I inclose in another wrapper the programme that Dewey has issued.[2] Mr. Quincy's note to me was to this effect "Mr. Evans has been here and I have arranged to send him my fathers Speeches &c by Express, so you need not send any of the copies you have kindly taken charge of to Indianapolis."[3] Sept. 18 was the date. You say "I am hereby authorized to draw upon you the Western agent for a copy of Quincy's Speeches." You will see these instructions do not tally. I have three copies of the Memoirs[4] to distribute but none of the Speeches. Perhaps he has sent through Osgood[5] some copies which I have not rec'd. You can have a copy when they arrive if you want one. You have heard from Miss Bean[6] of Lillie's engagement. The ladies of the household are much pleased with the arrangement. Annie is visiting for a month at Davenport, and Fred is in Wethersfield, Conn. I shall start for Phil. with Mrs. Poole Saturday noon, & we shall bring Fred back with [us]. He is growing up a nice boy.

You must go to Phil.

Yours very truly
W. F. Poole

I inclose with the programme 2 copies of the Chi. Lit. Club Scheme. Give one to Mr. Howland.[7]

ALS, *Evans Papers*, IUL.

[1]*Not located.*

[2]*Item 93.*

[3]*Josiah Quincy*, Speeches Delivered in the Congress of the United States . . . , *ed. by his son, Edmund Quincy. (Boston: Little, Brown, 1874). 412 p.*

[4]*Memoir of the Life of Josiah Quincy, junior, of Massachusetts, by his son, Josiah Quincy, 3rd ed. (Boston: Little, Brown, 1875). 431 p.*

[5]*Probably a reference to the Boston publisher, James R. Osgood (1836-1892).*

[6]*Mary Abbie Bean (1840-1893), Librarian, Brookline Public Library, 1871-1893.*

[7]*John D. Howland, friend of Evans and a founding member of the Indianapolis Literary Club, which was patterned after the Cincinnati and Chicago literary clubs.*

93. THE LIBRARY CONFERENCE (PROGRAMME)

[*Advance proofs from the* AMERICAN LIBRARY JOURNAL.]

THE LIBRARY CONFERENCE.

THE Conference of Librarians will assemble at the rooms of the Pennsylvania Historical Society on Wednesday, October 4th, 1876, at 10 o'clock, and, after a permanent organization has been effected, provision will be made for continuing the sessions by adjournment for the day and evening, so as to allow members an opportunity to devote a part of each day to the Exhibition grounds. If the attendance is larger than the rooms will accommodate, an adjournment will be made to the Lecture Room of the Franklin Institute, which has been tendered for that purpose. On Wednesday afternoon a visit will also be made by the Conference as a body to the new Ridgway (Rush) Library building, and in the evening the Conference will be entertained socially at the Historical rooms by the librarians of Philadelphia. During the sessions papers will be read as introductory to discussions on different subjects; and the various topics of library economy, as included in the special Report on Public Libraries issued by the Commissioner of Education will also be brought up for consideration. The following papers are already promised:

"A Universal Catalogue: its Necessity and Practicability." James G. Barnwell, Mercantile Library, Philadelphia.

"The Preservation of Pamphlets." Charles A. Cutter, Boston Athenæum.

"Personal Intercourse and Relations between Librarians and Readers in Popular Libraries." Samuel S. Green, Worcester Free Public Library.

"Bibliography as a Science." Reuben A. Guild, Librarian Brown University.

"The Modes of Construction appropriate to Public Libraries." S. F. Haven, American Antiquarian Society.

"Some Popular Objections to Public Libraries." William F. Poole, Chicago Public Library.

"Qualifications of a Librarian." Lloyd P. Smith, Philadelphia Library Company.

"Copyright in its Relations to Libraries and Literature." A. R. Spofford, Librarian of Congress.

"Helps to Reading." Justin Winsor, Superintendent Boston Public Library.

In addition to the topics in the Government Report there will be discussions on the following, among other subjects:

The Preparation of Printed Titles for the Common Use of Libraries.

The Completion of Poole's Index to Periodical Literature.

The Systematic Exchange of Duplicates.

The Distribution of Public Documents, home and foreign.

The Permanent Organization of American Library Interests.

Library Co-operation.

The Preparation of a Hand-Book for Readers suitable for Distribution in the Public Libraries.

Ideal *vs.* Working Libraries in our Universities.

The Committee expect to see a large gathering; and would renew the invitation to all librarians, both at home and abroad, and to all now or in the past in any way connected with libraries, and to all who may be interested in library economy or bibliographical studies.

JUSTIN WINSOR, Boston Public Library,
WM. F. POOLE, Chicago Public Library,
LLOYD P. SMITH, Philadelphia Library Co.,
Committee.

MELVIL DEWEY, *Secretary*
13 Tremont Place, Boston.

LIBRARY CO. OF PHILADELPHIA,
Fifth Street, below Chestnut,
Philadelphia, Sept. 9, 1876.

My DEAR SIR:

I am glad that Philadelphia has been selected as the place of meeting for the librarians of America, and I can assure you that the gentlemen who shall honor us by their presence will be heartily welcomed here. The directors of the Mercantile Library have passed a resolution throwing open their rooms to the members of the Convention, and I need not say that the Philadelphia and Loganian Libraries will extend a like hospitality.

In addition to the meetings in the morning it is proposed, on the afternoon of Tuesday, the 4th October, to visit in a body the new library building now in course of erection by the executor of the late Dr. James Rush. It occupies a square of ground on South Broad street, and will cost in all some $800,000. The architect sends you a description of it.

The building is entirely fire-proof, and will be finished and ready for occupation in about a year from the present time. It will then, by the direction of the testator, be formally offered for the acceptance of the Library Company of Philadelphia, under the title of the Ridgway Branch of the Philadelphia Library.

On some one evening during the sitting of the Convention, it is proposed to have a reception at the Historical Society's rooms for social intercourse, and to enable the members to make acquaintances among the literary gentlemen of Philadelphia.

My friends John Jordan, Jr. Esq., of the Historical Society, and James G. Barnwell, Esq., of the Mercantile Library, desire me to say that they unite with me in giving a cordial welcome to the gentlemen of the Convention, and that they will do all in their power to make the meeting an agreeable one.

I remain, my dear Mr. Dewey,

Yours very truly,

LLOYD P. SMITH.

MR. MELVIL DEWEY,
Sec. Library Conference Committee.

[*The* JOURNAL, *with local and other information as to the Conference, will be mailed to about 2000 libraries on Saturday night.*]

Printed document. This program, in the form of advance proofs from the first issue of the *American Library Journal,* was distributed before September 25, 1876, since Poole included a copy in his letter to Evans of that date. However, at least one conference member, Reuben A. Guild, had still not received his copy by September 30 (item 97). This is the last item in the 1876 scrapbook. Only Haven's paper was not read, though papers of Charles Evans and H. A. Homes were later added. The Saturday night mailing of the *Journal* to which this document refers was undoubtedly September 23, 1876. (See notes on item 95.) According to chronology, this would have been the fourth document (including the preliminary call) mailed to prospective conference members.

94. *WINSOR TO DEWEY*

PUBLIC LIBRARY, Boston Sept. 26, 1876

Shall leave Boston Friday P.M. and pass Sunday with a friend near Phil. and be at Smith's on Monday.

J. W.

Postcard, signed.

95. *GREEN TO DEWEY*

FREE PUBLIC LIBRARY
Worcester, Mass. Sept. 27, 1876

My dear Mr. Dewey.

Are there special rates for persons attending the Conference for railroad fare?

I am likely to start from Worcester, and go to Philadelphia [by] the New York & New England route or by the Boston & Albany railroad.

I have deferred asking you this question, thinking particulars would be given in the first number of the Library Journal.

I have not received this, however, and so return to make inquiry of you.

I, also, look forward with anticipation of pleasure in making your acquaintance at Philadelphia.

Truly yours
Samuel S. Green

ALS. Dewey's shorthand reply: "The Journal was to have been mailed last Saturday night [Sept. 23] but the printers have failed us so that it was delayed. It is promised today. We shall not get any better rates than the Centennial fares as our people go by so many different routes and times. Shall hope for you Wednesday morning." Dewey reported the same thing in ALJ, 1 (Sept. 30, 1876), 17.

96. AMERICAN LIBRARY JOURNAL—
EDITORIAL, SEPT. 30, 1876

The Committee's programme for the Philadelphia Conference is printed elsewhere. It will be seen that discussions on the more important library topics will be opened by papers from the leading librarians of the country. The history of the Conference is quickly told. Taking the hint from the meeting of 1853, a few library devotees in May last proposed a like gathering in connection with the great Exhibition. Letters of inquiry called out hearty responses from prominent librarians and the Commissioner of Education, and a preliminary call was issued.[1] It was at first proposed to hold the gathering in August, but the replies to the call generally agreed upon October as the better date, Philadelphia as the place, and Messrs. Winsor, Poole, and Smith as the proper committee to take charge of the arrangements. Announcement was made through the press, and the Bureau of Education forwarded the call to the libraries of this country and to the leading librarians abroad, and the responses to the invitation have been so general as to surprise even the projectors of the Conference. There will be a large attendance from all parts of this country, and delegates are also expected from Europe, Mr. Yates, of Leeds, for instance, being granted a considerable leave of absence for the purpose. The Conference affords opportunity to visit the Exhibition in the most favorable month; and the special Centennial fares, with reduced hotel terms procured by the Committee, make the trip comparatively inexpensive. There is no lack of inducement for librarians to attend; and as it should be the most profitable three days of their library life, it is scarcely to be supposed that any Board will refuse to grant leave of absence. Not the least important outcome of this meeting should be the proposed national organization. It is intended to give up the second number of the LIBRARY JOURNAL to a detailed report of the Conference.

Editorial, almost certainly by Melvil Dewey, in ALJ, 1 (Sept. 30, 1876), 13-14. Bowker, "The Library Journal and Library Organization: A Twenty Years' Retrospect," LJ, (Jan., 1896), p. 6, states that he and Dewey wrote the editorial section. The *Journal* was apparently mailed to subscribers just prior to their starting for Philadelphia. Bowker stated that the first number was published previous to the Conference, ALJ, 19 (June, 1894), [191] and Fleming, *R. R. Bowker*, p. 60, that it was available for distribution at the Conference. Guild expressed a hope to see the first issue on Sept. 30 (item 97). Beswick, *The Work of Frederick Leypoldt*, p. 54, quotes Dewey as stating that the first issue came from the press during the sessions of the Philadelphia Conference. No mention of its distribution at the conference is made in the proceedings. There is a brief notice of ALJ's appearance in *The World* (New York), Oct. 9, 1876, p. 2.

[1]*Item 29.*

97. GUILD TO DEWEY

Sept. 30. 76.

My dear Dewey

Have seen no circular yet, i.e. no copy sent to me.[1] Mr. Hedge[2] had a copy from which I made up a notice for the [Providence] Journal a copy of which I send you herewith.[3]

Hope to see the Library Journal to-night. Have finally decided to attend the conference "hit or miss." Shall leave here Tues. night and get in Phila. as soon as the cars will take me. Doubtful about my being there at the hour for organization.

> In haste
> Yours fraternally
> R. A. Guild

ALS.

[1]*Apparent reference to conference program. See 93.*

[2]*Josiah Dunham Hedge (1809-1879), Librarian, Providence, R.I., Athenæum, 1854-1879.*

[3]*Not located.*

98. HAVEN TO PRESIDING OFFICE OF THE LIBRARY CONFERENCE

AMERICAN ANTIQUARIAN SOCIETY
Worcester, Mass., Sept. 30, 1876

Dear Sir:

A combination of circumstances, partly personal, but more especially connected with official duties at home, renders it impracticable for me to attend the meeting of the librarians.

I am also prevented from completing the paper I had, on brief notice, proposed to offer, and I am unwilling to present an imperfectly prepared essay to such an audience.

It would have afforded me great gratification to meet a fraternity of which I have the honor to be a member (now, I believe, one of the oldest), and to have partaken of the pleasures and advantages of the Conference. I must, however, leave that enjoyment to my younger associate, Mr. Edmund M. Barton, Assistant Librarian, who will represent the Library of the American Antiquarian Society, and extend its right hand of fellowship to other institutions. I beg permission to commend him as a most worthy member of our faculty.

Very faithfully yours,
S. F. Haven

Printed letter, read at the conference. ALJ, 1 (Nov. 30, 1876), 101.

99. WILLIAM DUNN MACRAY TO DEWEY

DUCKLINGTON RECTORY
Whitney
Oxfordshire
Oct. 2, 1876

Sir,

In the month of August last I received a circular[1] posted at Manchester in this country, but endorsed as coming from the Washington Bureau of Education, inviting me to attend a Conference of Librarians to be held at Philadelphia in the present week. As no address was given to which a reply was to be sent, I did not then send any acknowledgement, but I hope it is not even now too late to convey to you, as Secretary of the Conference, my thanks for the communication, and to express the pleasure which it would have given me to attend your meeting, had it been at all possible for me to do so. Having been all my life engaged in bibliographical pursuits, the objects of your Conference possess great interest for me, and I trust that its proceedings will (by the time you receive this) have passed off in a very satisfactory & successful manner.

I beg to remain, Sir, your faithful Servant

> Will. Dunn Macray M.A.
> Assistant Librarian of the
> Bodleian Library, Oxford

ALS. Dewey's shorthand reply at top peculiarly says "Write Edwards," presumably Edward Edwards. William Dunn Macray (1826-1916), spent all his professional life in various capacities in the Bodleian Library.

[1] *Item 62, which the Bureau forwarded, probably through the American consulate.*

100. *LIBRARIANS' CONVENTION*

LIBRARIANS' CONVENTION

The Librarians of the City of Philadelphia request the pleasure of your company, on Friday Evening, Oct. 6, 1876, between the hours of 8 and 11, at the rooms of the Historical Society, No. 820 Spruce St.

PLEASE PRESENT THIS CARD AT THE DOOR

Invitation card. Mrs. Justin Winsor's copy. This is one of the last items in the Scrapbook. Preliminary announcements had indicated an entertainment on Wed., Oct. 4, 1876. The conference adjourned at about 1 p.m. on Oct. 6. "In the evening the librarians, with other literary gentlemen and ladies of Philadelphia, received the visiting delegates at the rooms of the Historical Society. The evening was spent in informal social intercourse, during which an elegant collation was served. And thus ended, with pleasant words and good cheer, the Centennial CONFERENCE OF LIBRARIANS." ALJ, 1 (Nov. 30, 1876), 143.

LIBRARIANS' CONVENTION.

The Librarians of the City of Philadelphia request the pleasure of your company, on Friday Evening, Oct. 6, 1876, between the hours of 8 and 11, at the rooms of the Historical Society, No. 820 Spruce St.

PLEASE PRESENT THIS CARD AT THE DOOR.

"The Pleasure of Your Company"

Index of Names

Abbot, Ezra, 37, 38, 54, 61, 80, 91
Arnold, Ebenezer Cary, 74, 75
Ashhurst, John, Jr., 65

Bailey, John Jay, 71, 83
Barnard, Frederick A. P., 37
Barnard, Henry, 18
Barnwell, James G., 47, 55, 61, 62, 72, 92, 107, 127, 129
Barton, Edmund Mills, 104, 135
Bean, Mary Abbie, 22, 126
Belden, Charles, xi
Billings, John Shaw, 18, 40, 55, 64, 65
Bonnange, Ferdinand, 60, 61
Bowker, Richard Rodgers, ix, 6, 7, 8, 9, 14, 16, 19, 20, 21, 22, 24, 25, 26, 27, 28, 29, 40, 55, 121, 133
Brevoort, James Carson, 50, 54, 91
Burley, George L., 81
Butler, Wentworth Sanborn, 49, 54, 92, 115

Carnes, Emily F., 12, 65, 66
Clark, S. N., 76, 84, 86, 87, 93
Clarke, Emma Leonore, 125
Crunden, Frederick M., 71
Cutter, Charles Ammi, xii, xiii, 4, 5, 8, 9, 11, 12, 13, 20, 21, 24, 35, 37, 38, 51, 52, 54, 80, 88, 91, 92, 102, 103, 105, 106, 120, 127

Dewey, Melvil, frontispiece, ix, x, xi, xiii, xiv, 3, 4, 5, 6, 7, 8, 9, 10, 11, 12, 13, 14, 15, 16, 17, 18, 19, 20, 21, 22, 24, 25, 26, 27, 28, 29, 30, 31, 32, 35, 36, 37, 38, 40, 41, 42, 44, 46, 49, 52, 53, 54, 55, 57, 58, 59, 60, 61, 63, 64, 65, 67, 68, 69, 70, 71, 72, 73, 74, 75, 76, 77, 79, 80, 84, 85, 86, 87, 88, 92, 93, 95, 97, 98, 99, 100, 101, 102, 103, 104, 105, 106, 107, 110, 112, 113, 114, 115, 116, 117, 118, 119, 120, 121, 122, 124, 125, 126, 128, 129, 131, 133, 134, 135, 136
Dexter, Franklin B., 55, 91

Of this book ten thousand copies have been printed on Warren's India Wove Old Style. With the exception of the title-page, the entire book is set in eleven-point monotype Baskerville. The book was produced at The Lakeside Press, R. R. Donnelley & Sons Company, Chicago, Illinois and Crawfordsville, Indiana.